THE GREAT BOOK OF CALIFORNIA

The Crazy History of California with Amazing Random Facts & Trivia

**A Trivia Nerds Guide
to the History of the
United States Vol.3**

BILL O'NEILL

ISBN-13: 978-1722057695

DON'T FORGET YOUR FREE BOOKS

CONTENTS

CHAPTER TWO

CHAPTER THREE
FACTS ABOUT CALIFORNIA'S

INTRODUCTION

How much do you know about the state of California?

Sure, you know it's home to Hollywood. You know the state has a lot of natural disasters, ranging from earthquakes to wildfires. But what else do you *really* know about the state?

You might know California has a huge population, but do you know how it got some of its population?

Have you ever wondered how California was named? Do you know how it came to be nicknamed the Golden State?

Do you know which celebrities have held government positions in California?

You know all about Hollywood. At least, you *think* you do. Do you know who drove the film industry to California in the first place? Do you know how much it costs to get your name on the Hollywood Walk of Fame?

Did you know Beverly Hills wasn't always a

community where the rich and famous lived? Do you know what it was before the glitz and glamour took over?

Do you know which popular toy originated from the state or which popular frozen treat was invented in California by accident?

Do you know which famous fast-food chain opened its first location in California?

Do you know about the celebrity sex icon whose death remains a mystery to this day?

Did you know California was once the murdering grounds for one of America's most famous serial killers? Do you know about the mysterious hotel death that went viral?

If you have ever wondered about the answers to these or other questions, then you're in luck! This book is filled with stories and facts about the state of California.

This isn't just any book about California. It will highlight some of the facts that have helped form the Golden State into what it is today. You'll learn facts about the state you've probably never even considered before. Once you're done reading, you'll know everything there is to know about California.

The state of California is rich in both its history and culture. While we'll try to stick to a timeline as we explore some of the state's most significant historical facts, we'll also jump around some.

This book is broken up into easy to follow chapters that will help you learn more about the Golden State. Once you have completed each chapter, you can test your knowledge with trivia questions!

Some of the facts you'll read about in this book are surprising. Others are sad, and some may even give you goosebumps. But the one thing all of these facts have in common, is that they're all fascinating. Once you've finished reading this book, you'll be an expert on the state of California.

The book will answer the following questions:

How did California get its name?

Why is it nicknamed the Golden State?

Why did filmmakers choose to open studios in Hollywood?

Which genres of music started out in California?

Which California-born celebrity sex icon's death remains a mystery?

Which fast-food chain got its start in California?

And so much more!

CHAPTER ONE

CALIFORNIA'S HISTORY AND RANDOM FACTS

California was the 31st state to join the United States. It's famous for the California Gold Rush, but did you know there was another rush that took place in the state? Do you know how the state got its name? Do you know what the official state animal is and why it's now extinct in the state? Do you know how California got its state nickname? Read on to find out the answers to these and other questions!

California Was Given Its Name by Mistake

Did you know California was mistakenly named?

When the Spanish first visited the area in 1533, they named the area "California," with lower California (now located in Mexico) being known as "Baja California" and upper California being called "Alta California." But what gave them the idea to name the region this in the first place?

The name "California" stemmed from a Spanish fictional romance novel called *Las Serges de Esplandian* by Garcia Ordonez de Montalvo, which was published in 1510. In the book, Montalvo described a mythical island paradise called Califia, where there were lots of pearls and gold.

Califia was a fictional place, but when early Spanish settlers found California in 1535, they believed they had actually found Califia. The area, they thought, resembled Califia, since they mistakenly believed the peninsula was an island. In addition, they found pearls.

The earliest maps of California depicted the peninsula to be an island. Francisco de Ulloa would later discover the early explorers' mistakes, but it was already too late. Since the name California had already been applied to the maps, the name stuck.

Spanish Missions Had Devastating Effects on California's Native Americans

The Spanish began a California missions program in 1769. A total of 21 missions were built throughout California. The purpose of these missions was to convert Native Americans to Catholicism, as well as expand Spanish territory throughout the state.

Native Americans were provided with both religious and cultural instruction. They would then be baptized. Afterward, men would generally go to work in the fields and women were put to work in the kitchen.

Once the Native Americans in one area had been converted to Catholicism, the mission would be converted into a church. The missionaries would then move on to the next location where they would begin converting more Native Americans.

The missions program was stopped in 1833, not long after Mexico won its independence from Spain. During this time, the territory of California was still under Mexican rule. It was already too late, however. The Spanish missions already had devastating effects on the Native American population.

The Spanish missionaries brought diseases with them that the Native Americans weren't immune to. Before the California missions program began in 1794, it's been estimated that there were 300,000 Native Americans residing in the state—and only about 20,000 by 1834.

In addition, many of the Native Americans' cultures and traditions were lost during the process. Some have compared the California missions to slave or concentration camps. Prostitution is said to have occurred during those times.

In 1865, Abraham Lincoln granted the Catholic Church some of the buildings that were originally used as missions. Many of these structures can still be found today.

California Was Once a Country of Its Own

Did you know that California was actually its own

country at one point?

During the 1840s, settlers moved to California from the east using the Oregon Trail and the California Trail. Once they arrived, the settlers began to rebel against Mexican rule.

In 1846, John Fremont led settlers to revolt against the Mexican government. They declared California an independent country, which they called both the California Republic and, less formally, the Bear Republic. They flew a flag they made, which consisted of a lone star and a hand-drawn grizzly bear, over the country.

The Bear Republic was short-lived, lasting for less than a month. The rebels didn't realize the United States had already declared war on Mexico. The Bear Republic gave up its independence and pledged its allegiance to the United States.

When the Mexican-American War ended in 1848, the United States managed to claim the territory of California. The Treaty of Guadalupe Hidalgo marked the end of the war. The United States paid Mexico $15 million in war damages. In exchange, Mexico gave the USA half of its territory, which included California (along with Arizona, Texas, and New Mexico, as well as parts of Colorado, Nevada, and Utah).

In 1850, California officially became a part of the Union.

In recent years, there have been talks about California becoming a country of its own again due to the state having views more liberal than most of the U.S. Is it possible for this to happen? According to *Constitution Daily*, a new constitutional amendment *could* make it possible for California to secede from the union and give the United States its own "Brexit." California would need to receive permission from the other 49 states. Will this ever actually happen? Time will tell!

You Can Thank the Gold Rush for California's Population

California is the state with the highest population in the USA. In fact, approximately one out of every eight United States residents lives in California. As of 2008, the state was estimated to be home to nearly 40 million people, which is more than the number of people living in the entire country of Canada. But did you know the Gold Rush is the reason California's population grew to begin with?

In 1848, James Marshall discovered gold at Sutter's Mill in Coloma, California. As a result, tens of thousands of people set out to California in hopes of getting rich. Between the years of 1848 and 1855, more than 300,000 people migrated to California. They came from the eastern United States, as well as other countries. It was the largest mass migration to ever take place in the history of the United States.

The California Gold Rush is also what helped turn San Francisco into the city it is today. What had started out as a small fishing village of 200 people became the now well-known city of San Francisco when it gained 35,000 new residents. Today, the city has an estimated population of nearly 900,000.

And it's no wonder! Between the years of 1850 and 1859, more than 28 million ounces of gold was extracted from California.

Although it was what first sparked interest in the state, the gold rush wasn't the only thing that drew people to the Golden State. When the California Gold Rush ended, people didn't stop migrating to California. In 1869, the First Transcontinental Railroad helped increase travel to the state. In addition, California became a major state for farming crops like grapes, almonds, tomatoes, and more. People saw it as a place for farms and wineries to thrive.

California Also Had a Silver Rush

California is generally associated with the gold rush and Nevada is known for its silver rush. But did you know that California had a silver rush of its own?

Calico in San Bernardino County is the town most often associated with California's silver rush. The town was established in 1881 when the largest amount of silver was found in California. Calico was home to about 500 mines. During the 12 years that people worked in the mines, more than $20 million in silver came out of Calico.

When the price of silver ended up dropping by more than half its value, the residents of Calico left the town. By 1904, Calico was a ghost town. By the 1950s, the town was purchased by Walter Knott, who founded Knott's Berry Farm. Knott preserved what was left of the town to turn it into a tourist attraction. He later donated Calico to San Bernardino County.

Today, Calico is a historical landmark and makes up part of a regional park. It's now known as "California's Silver Rush Ghost Town." It's a popular tourist attraction, visited by people from all over the world!

The Discovery of Oil Helped Shape Los Angeles Into the City it is Today

With an estimated population of more than 3.9 million, Los Angeles is one of the most populated cities in America today. Did you know it was once just a small town? In fact, in 1820, Los Angeles was only home to 620 residents.

It wasn't until oil was discovered in 1892 near today's Dodger Stadium that Los Angeles began to gain recognition. Over time, more oil was discovered throughout the city. In fact, by 1923, Los Angeles was producing 25% of the world's petroleum.

After oil was discovered, Los Angeles's population began to increase. By the 1900 census, it had grown to 100,000 people. By 1960, there were more than 2 million people residing in the city.

Even to this day, Los Angeles remains a large producer of oil. There are still over 3,000 oil and gas wells in the city that are active today. The majority of these wells are located in residential communities and retailer developments. One oil well located on the property of Beverly Hills High School produces 400 barrels daily and earns about $300,000 a year.

The Golden State Wasn't California's First State Nickname

California was nicknamed the Golden State due to both the gold rush and its golden poppies, which bloom in spring throughout the state. It's also been said that the sun may play a role in its current nickname. But did you know that California wasn't always known as the Golden State? It actually had another nickname first!

California was originally nicknamed the Grizzly Bear State due to its high population of grizzly bears in the early 1800s. It's been estimated that there were tens of thousands of the bears in the state during those times. When the human population increased, its grizzly bear population was killed off. The last grizzly bear in the state was killed in the early 1920s.

Today, the grizzly bear is the official state animal of California. It's the only state with an official state animal that no longer exists in the state.

Although the idea of featuring a grizzly bear on the California state flag came about when the rebels gained control, the grizzly bear on the current state flag is Monarch. Monarch was a 1,200-pound wild grizzly bear from California who was captured by a reporter named Allen Kelley. Monarch lived out the rest of his life as a star attraction at Woodward's Garden in San Francisco and later at the Golden Gate Park.

The Bubonic Plague Epidemic in the U.S. First Broke Out in San Francisco's Chinatown

In the early 1900s, the bubonic plague began to make its way through the United States. Did you know the disease started out in California?

In 1899, a ship that sailed from Hong Kong to San Francisco was carrying two passengers with the bubonic plague. The plague was expected to be quarantined when the ship arrived on Angel Island. However, two stowaways managed to escape the ship. Both were found dead in the Bay area, and their bodies tested positive for the plague.

While the bubonic plague didn't immediately strike the city, it's believed that rats aboard the ship were probably responsible for the outbreak.

In March of 1900, a Chinese man's deceased body tested positive for the plague. An anti-Chinese movement took place, causing Chinatown to be quarantined. The quarantine was eventually lifted because it was bad for business, but people in Chinatown were subject to home inspections. There was a lot of resistance throughout the community, with people locking their doors or hiding dead bodies.

When two more bubonic plague victims were found dead, the San Francisco City Board of Health announced the plague's presence in the city. With President McKinley's permission, anti-plague initiatives were taken. By 1903, 122 people in San Francisco and surrounding areas had died.

In 1905, researchers confirmed that the bubonic plague was spread when fleas from infected rats bit humans.

The bubonic plague began to spread again following the 1906 San Francisco Earthquake. There was a large rat and flea infestation when people were living in the refugee camps following the disaster. This time, the bubonic plague spread even more rampantly before it ended in 1909.

The Deadliest Earthquake in the U.S. Took Place in California in 1906

You probably already know that California is known for its earthquakes. It's been estimated that there are approximately 10,000 earthquakes each year, but only about 15 to 20 of those reach a magnitude higher than 4.0. Unfortunately, thousands of lives have been lost in the Golden State as a result of earthquakes, however. In fact, the 1906 San Francisco Earthquake was the deadliest earthquake in U.S. history.

The earthquake, with a moment magnitude believed to be 7.9, struck at 5:12 a.m. on April 18th, 1906. Tremors were felt in surrounding areas. This caused devastating fires to break out in San Francisco. The fires lasted several days. They caused more damage than the earthquake itself. More than 80% of San Francisco was destroyed in the disaster.

Only 375 deaths were reported in San Francisco and throughout the bay area at the time. However, there were hundreds of fatalities in Chinatown that went undocumented. Although no one knows for certain how many people died during the 1906 San Francisco Earthquake, it's been estimated that there were up to 3,000 fatalities.

The number of lives lost in the disaster was the highest of any natural disaster in the history of California. The death toll also ranks high on the lists of disasters to have ever taken place in an American city.

In addition to the lives lost, between 227,000 and 300,000 people (out of about 410,000 affected) were left without homes. Refugee camps were set up in Golden Gate Park, the Panhandle, the Presidio, and across beaches. The camps remained there for more than two years.

The 1906 earthquake makes history for another reason, too. It's the first significant natural disaster that was ever documented in photographs and video recordings.

California Sterilized More People Through Its State-Run Eugenics Program Than Any Other U.S. State

Are you ready to hear about one of the most tragic things that have ever occurred in the history of California?

You may have heard of state-run eugenics programs, in which people were involuntarily sterilized. The idea was to prevent selected people from having children to eliminate society of people considered "defective." Thirty-two U.S. states had sterilization programs, but California's was, by far, the largest.

In 1909, California passed a sterilization law. It was the third state to do so. The law gave superintendents at state-run institutions permission to involuntarily sterilize patients who were found to be too "unfit" or "feebleminded." Males were given vasectomies against their will, while women were given salpingectomies (or fallopian tube removal).

Most of these sterilizations took place at state-run mental institutions, but they also took place in state prisons. People who were chosen to be sterilized were chosen due to a number of possible reasons. Patients could be sterilized for being mentally ill, handicapped, sexually deviant, homosexual, and criminals, to name a few of the many reasons.

Superintendents got to make the decisions, and there was no way for the young men and women who were sterilized to appeal their decisions. Most of them didn't even find out they were going to be sterilized until it was actually happening. Some were never even told by the facilities they were in what had happened.

The sterilization program was racially charged. In recent times, researchers have discovered that people with Spanish surnames were 2.5 times as likely to be sterilized than those without. Mexican immigrants were especially affected due to stereotyping. Mexican men were considered to be criminals, while Mexican women were believed to be hypersexual and would have too many children if they weren't sterilized.

Coercion was also used in some sterilization cases.

Patients were sometimes given the option to leave the state-run institution they were at if they agreed to be sterilized.

It's been estimated that about 20,000 people were involuntarily sterilized in California between the years of 1909 and 1979. This makes up about one-third of all people involuntarily sterilized in the United States.

California's eugenics program was so large and considered to be so effective that the Nazi party in Germany even used it as a model for their own sterilization program.

In 1979, former California senator Art Torres, wrote the legislation outlawing sterilization.

Although sterilization is believed to be a thing of the past, it's been estimated that nearly 150 women were sterilized in state prisons between 2006 and 2010.

California's Wine Industry Took a Huge Hit During the Prohibition

Today, California is known for its wine industry. The Golden State grows over 3 million tons of wine grapes every year. The state produces approximately 90% of all wine in the United States, with 17 million gallons being produced annually. But did you know California's wine industry was once impacted by the Prohibition? In fact, the impact of the law devastated wineries.

Before we go into how the Prohibition affected California's wine industry, let's start from the very beginning.

California's wine industry dates all the way back to 1796 when Spanish Franciscan Missionaries planted vineyards in order to have wine for communion. The first variety of grapes planted in the earliest vineyards was known as the Mission grape and remained the most common variety until the 1880s.

In the early 1830s, vineyards were planted in Southern California. Jean-Louis Vignes and William Wolfskill, two of the earliest major wine producers, planted their first vineyards in Los Angeles.

As people began to migrate to California during the gold rush, the demand for wine increased. Vineyards began to increase throughout the state. They were planted throughout Northern California in Napa County, El Dorado County, Sonoma County, and Sutter County (which are home to some of the most famous California vineyards today).

By the 1900s, the booming California wine industry was recognized throughout the entire world. The state was exporting wine to England, Australia, Central America, and Asia.

There were more than 700 wineries in California by

the time the Prohibition was passed in 1919. One of the loopholes of the Prohibition allowed people to produce up to "200 gallons of non-intoxicating cider and fruit juice" in their homes. People began making wine in their homes, causing grape sales—and prices—to soar. Vineyards began to produce low-quality grapes that were easier to ship.

By the end of the prohibition in 1933, less than 100 wineries throughout the entire United States had managed to stay afloat. It took more than 50 years for California's wine industry to return to the way it was prior to the Prohibition.

Today, California is known for producing some of the best wines in the entire world!

California Was the First State to Ban Marijuana

You probably already know that California was the first state to legalize medical marijuana. The law, which was passed in 1996, encouraged other states to eventually follow suit. Today, the use of marijuana for both medicinal and recreational purposes is legal in California. But did you know that California didn't always have such a liberal stance on marijuana? In fact, California was the first state to ban marijuana back in 1913.

In 1907, the Poison Act, which declared cannabis to be a poison, was passed in California. In 1913, an

Walt Disney Got His Inspiration for Disneyland at a Los Angeles Park

Walt Disney's daughters, Sharon and Diane, were riding the merry-go-round at Griffith Park in Los Angeles when he came up with the idea of an amusement park that could be enjoyed by adults and their children. The idea evolved when fans asked to visit the Walt Disney Studios, which he knew didn't have much to offer them.

Opening the park was easier said than done, however. Walt Disney found it difficult to find investors for the park. Most people, including his brother Roy Disney, thought the project would only end in ruin. Walt ended up creating a show called *Disneyland*, which aired on the ABC network. In exchange, the network funded the park. ABC was responsible for one-third of the $17 million it took to build the park. Walt ended up going to other extreme means to find funds, such as borrowing against his life insurance and selling his vacation properties.

Walt originally planned to open the park in Burbank, California, but Harrison Price from Stanford Research Institute advised him to build the park in Anaheim instead. Walt acquired a 160-acre plot of land that originally housed orange groves and walnut trees.

Walt originally planned to call his theme park Disneylandia, but ABC recommended that he go with

Disneyland instead. When excavation of the site began, Walt decided to go with ABC's name recommendation.

The park opened in 1955, which had a huge impact on Anaheim. The city, which was originally a rural farming community, experienced rapid growth with the opening of Disneyland. Hotels and residential communities made their way to the area. Anaheim also became an industrial hub. Electronics, aircraft parts, and canned fruit also began to be produced in the area.

Several Actors Have Gone into Politics in California

Did you know that three actors have held political positions in California?

Ronald Reagan served as the 40th President of the United States between the years of 1981 and 1989. Prior to winning the presidential election, he was the Governor of California from 1967 to 1974. But before he even started a career in politics, Ronald Reagan was a popular actor. Many people have attributed his popularity in the film industry and his good looks as the reason he was ever elected into politics at all. Ronald Reagan starred in movies like *Cattle Queen of Montana*, *Hellcats of the Navy*, and *The Girl from Jones Beach*.

Clint Eastwood is well-known for his career in the film industry, but did you know he had a brief stint in politics? The actor rose to fame after he starred in *The Man with No Name* and the *Dirty Harry* films. He later went on to direct numerous films, including *Million Dollar Baby*. But did you know that between 1986 and 1988, Clint Eastwood served as the mayor of Carmel-by-the-Sea in California?

Actor Arnold Schwarzenegger served as the Governor of California between 2003 and 2011. Prior to his political career, Schwarzenegger was best-known for his role in *The Terminator* film series. Though Schwarzenegger has talked about a possible presidential run in the future, his plans seem to have been derailed by accusations of sexual misconduct and a messy divorce from Maria Shriver.

RANDOM FACTS

1. The capital of the Golden State has changed more than once. When California first joined the union, the capital was San Jose. The capital was later moved to Vallejo and then Benicia before Sacramento was chosen as the state capital in 1854. Sacramento had an ideal geographical location for the state's capital. Since it's not located near an ocean, the chances of an invasion were low. Sacramento was also a popular destination for new settlers due to the gold rush.

2. California's state motto is, "Eureka!" The motto came about during the gold rush. It's been said that "Eureka!"—which means "I have found it!" in Greek—was said by Greek mathematician Archimedes when he found a method to determine the purity of gold.

3. Before it was named San Francisco, the city was known as something else first. It was originally called Yerba Buena, meaning "good herb" in Spanish.

4. Three of the 10 most populated cities in the United States are located in California. They are (in order): Los Angeles, San Diego, and San Jose. San Francisco, Fresno, Sacramento, Long Beach, and Oakland all fall into the top 50 most populated

cities in America, according to moving.com.

5. The majority of California's residents are minorities. More than half of its population is made up of Asians, Hispanics, Native Americans, and other minority groups. More than 25% of California's residents were born outside of America. San Francisco is home to the second largest Chinatown outside of Asia and the largest Japantown in the United States.

6. Beverly Hills is one of the most famous neighborhoods in Los Angeles. Today, it's best known for its high-value real estate and Hollywood movie star residents, both past, and present. But before it became known for its stardom and glamour, Beverly Hills started out as a lima bean ranch. Back in the 1800s, the land was owned and used to grow lima beans by business partners Andrew H. Henker and Henry Hammel. When it became a housing development in 1906, it was named after Beverly Farms and the hills of Beverly, Massachusetts. The first house was built in Beverly Hills in 1907. The development was planned to be an all-white community. People in Beverly Hills weren't allowed to sell or rent their homes to Jews.

7. During the stock market crash of 1929, thousands of banks in the United States failed. In 1933, there were only 11,000 banks remaining in the country.

All of San Francisco's banks survived the stock market crash. In fact, the economy was so good in the region that construction of the Golden Gate Bridge began at that time.

8. Angel Island is thought of as the "Ellis Island of the West." It was used between 1910 and 1940. Unlike the more relaxed Ellis Island, immigrants were detained for days to months before they were allowed entry into the country. While the majority of the 1-3% who were rejected from entering into the country through Angel Island were Chinese, it's been estimated that 175,000 Asian immigrants entered the United States through the immigration station. Today, Angel Island is a state park and national historical landmark.

9. Like other U.S. states, California has a number of strange laws. Throughout the entire state, a vehicle may not surpass 60 mph without a driver. In Fresno, it's illegal to annoy a lizard in a public park. In Los Angeles County, you cannot throw a frisbee without a lifeguard's permission. In Dana Point, it's illegal to use your own bathroom while the window's open. In San Francisco, you're not allowed to store things in your garage. In Pacific Grove, it's illegal to "mess with, molest, or hunt" butterflies. California's odd laws don't stop at humans, either. Animals cannot mate within 1,500

feet of a place of worship, tavern or school.

10. When it was first founded, Los Angeles was originally known as "El Pueblo de Nuestra Senora Reina de los Angeles sobre le Rio Porciuncula." The Spanish meaning of this is "the town of our lady queen of the angels on the Porciuncula River." Today, Los Angeles is simply known as "The City of Angels."

11. The largest county in the United States can be found in California. San Bernardino County takes up nearly 3 million acres of space. It encompasses more land than four U.S. states combined (New Jersey, Rhode Island, Connecticut, and Delaware).

12. The Great Flood of California took place between Christmas Eve of 1861 through the end of January of 1862. It rained almost continually during these time periods. The Central Valley turned into an inland sea, nearly 25% of the state's property was destroyed, and the state went bankrupt.

13. Wildfire season in California takes place between early summer and October. In Southern California, however, wildfire season is considered to be year-round due to chronically worse drought conditions in the region.

14. While Ladies Nights are a popular pastime throughout much of the United States, they're illegal in California. The reason? Gender

discrimination.

15. Former United States President Richard Nixon is from Yorba Linda, California. He grew up in Whittier, California. After his older brother died of tuberculosis while attending Whittier High School, his parents sent him to Fullerton Union High School, which was an hour away. He attended Whittier College before eventually going to Duke University School of Law. Nixon was elected to the U.S. House of Representatives and served as the Senator of California before serving as Vice President and eventually as the 36th President of the United States.

16. Blue Diamond, which is located in Sacramento, is the world-leading almond producer. The plant produces over 12 million pounds of almonds per year.

17. "The Country Store" in Baker, California has sold more winning lottery tickets than any other store in the state.

18. La Jolla, California was originally named "La Joya" by early Spanish settlers. This translates into "the jewel." It's also been said that La Jolla was called "the land of holes" by the local Kumeyaay due to the city's sea caves. Rumor has it that pirates once used those sea caves to smuggle in contraband and other goods.

19. During the California Gold Rush, treasure hunters would sail into the San Francisco harbor and leave their ships abandoned. These ships were later used to build houses and businesses in the region.

20. The second largest natural disaster in the history of California was the collapse of the St. Francis Dam. Within two years of being built, the dam ruptured, causing water to engulf entire towns. It's been estimated that somewhere between 400 and 600 lives were lost in the natural disaster.

Test Yourself – Questions and Answers

1. The name California stemmed from what mythical island in a 1950 Spanish romance novel?

    a. Fornia
    b. Cali
    c. Califia

2. California's population boom wiped out which animal?

    a. Black bears
    b. Grizzly bears
    c. Cougars

3. The film industry moved to Hollywood to escape which famous person?

    a. Thomas Edison
    b. Albert Einstein
    c. Walt Disney

4. Beverly Hills originally started out as a _____.

    a. Avocado farm
    b. Lima bean ranch
    c. Almond grove

5. Which actor has not held a political position in California?

    a. Arnold Schwarzenegger
    b. Clint Eastwood
    c. Robert DeNiro

Answers

1. c.
2. b.
3. a.
4. b.
5. c.

CHAPTER TWO

CALIFORNIA'S POP CULTURE

California is a state that's rich in pop culture, which is no surprise since it's home to Hollywood. Have you ever wondered what famous people got their start in California? Which famous children's author lived in the state? What genre of music originated from the Golden State? What famous late iconic actress came from California? Read on to find out the answers to these and other random facts about California's pop culture!

How Hollywood Got Its Name

While it is a place, the term "Hollywood" is used to refer to anyone or anything regarding show business today. Have you ever wondered how Hollywood got its name?

H.J. Whitley, the Father of Hollywood and developer of the town, was the one who gave it its name.

There have been several different theories about why he chose the name. Some believe he picked the name due to a bush found in the area that closely resembles holly.

According to Whitley's diary, however, there was another reason he chose the name. One day, he came across an Asian man who was pulling wood in a wagon. The man told him, "I holly wood" to explain he was hauling wood. This inspired Whitley to name the town Hollywood— "holly" in honor of England and "wood" for his own Scottish origin.

Regardless of how the town was named, it's hard to imagine the world without Hollywood today!

The Rise and Fall of West Coast Hip Hop

West Coast hip hop originated in Los Angeles in the mid-1970s. Alonzo Williams from Compton, California began to DJ parties using the name the "Wreckin' Cru." Both he and another DJ named Rodger Clayton who deejayed under Uncle Jamm's Army began to host large parties at nightclubs.

Unlike East Coast hip hop, West Coast hip hop had stronger electronic music influences and was faster paced. West coast hip hop focused more on DJing than rapping. Breakdancing was invented as a result of West Coast hip hop, which also set it apart from East Coast hip hop.

Perhaps one of the most well-known albums to come out of the genre was *Straight Outta Compton*, which was put out by the group N.W.A in 1988. The members of the group included Dr. Dre, Ice Cube,

Eazy-E, and MC Ren. In the 1990s, all of the members later went on to become platinum-selling solo artists.

Tupac Shakur's first album, titled *2Pacalypse Now*, came out in 1991. It quickly rose to popularity due to its focus on social injustice and police brutality. Tupac received a lot of critical acclaim for his music, which drew attention to West Coast hip hop.

The following year, Death Row Records put out Dr. Dre's first album, and his single "Nuthin' but a 'G' Thang" hit No. 2 on the *Billboard* Hot 100. The record company also saw success with Snoop Doggy Dogg's *Doggystyle* and 2Pac's *All Eyez on Me*.

There's no doubt that scandal in the hip hop industry helped increase West Coast hip hop's popularity. An East-West Coast feud between Puff Daddy and The Notorious B.I.G. of Bad Boy Records and Death Row Records and Tupac had been going on throughout the 1990s. The feud garnered a lot of publicity when Tupac Shakur was shot in 1994 while Biggie Smalls and Puff Daddy had been recording. Tupac accused Puff Daddy and Biggie Smalls of setting him up.

The hip hop industry as a whole was forever changed when Tupac was murdered in a drive-by shooting in 1996. Around the same time, Suge Knight, founder of Death Row Records, went to prison. The loss of the record company's founder and biggest musician led to the death of Death Row Records.

The East-West Coast feud ended when the Notorious B.I.G. was killed in a drive-by shooting. It was around this time that the popularity of the West Coast hip hop scene fell. Fans began to listen to the new East Coast hip hop artists, such as 50 Cent.

Other Music Genres Got Their Start in California

Surf music got its start in Southern California. It's a genre of rock music that's often associated with surf culture. Surf music came to be in the late 1950s and really blew up in the early 1960s. There were two different types of surf music: instrumental and vocal. Dick Dale was the most popular instrumental surf music artist, while the Beach Boys led the vocal side of the genre.

Third wave ska is another genre that started out in California. Third wave ska was popular with the punk culture scene during the late 1980s and became commercially successful in the 1990s. Some of the most popular bands included the Mighty Mighty Bostones, Reel Big Fish, Goldfinger, and Less Than Jake. The genre gained popularity when the band called the Donkey Show picked up steam in San Diego and went on to tour the rest of the state.

There were a number of other genres of music that grew in popularity thanks to bands who came out of California.

Heavy metal grew in popularity with the rise of Los Angeles-based band Metallica.

Pop punk also gained a large following thanks to the band Green Day, which originated from East Bay, California.

A Library in San Diego Honors Dr. Seuss's Legacy

Theodore Seuss Geisel, better known for his pseudonym "Dr. Seuss", lived in La Jolla, California.

Geisel and his wife Helen moved to La Jolla after World War II ended. During the war, Geisel drew political cartoons and later drew posters to directly support the U.S. war effort. It wasn't until Geisel moved to La Jolla that he began to write the famous children's books many of us have come to love.

While living in La Jolla, Geisel wrote *Green Eggs and Ham*, *The Cat in the Hat*, *Horton Hears a Who!*, *How the Grinch Stole Christmas!*, and other fan favorites.

Geisel died in 1991, but San Diego still honors Dr. Seuss's legacy. You can visit the University of California, San Diego's Geisel Library, which is home to the largest collection of original manuscripts, photos, drawings, and other artifacts. While the artifacts are preserved for most of the year, there's a Dr. Seuss exhibit held during the author's birth month (March) and during the summer months. There's also a Dr. Seuss and *Cat in the Hat* statue outside of the Geisel Library.

In Scripps Park in La Jolla, you can see the Monterrey Cypress tree that inspired Dr. Seuss's Lorax trees. Geisel was able to view the tree from the observatory at his home in La Jolla.

A 1990s Cult Classic Movie Centered on Beverly Hills

A 1990s film with a strong cult following took place in Beverly Hills. The movie *Clueless*, which was released in 1995, centered on a teenager named Cher growing up in the upscale community.

Cher was played by California native actress Alicia Silverstone, but she wasn't the first choice for the film. Sarah Michelle Gellar and Reese Witherspoon were both considered for the role.

Cher's house in the movie is supposed to be located at 901 Drury Lane in Beverly Hills. While this is an actual address, the mansion featured in the movie is actually located in the Valley. Her best friend Dionne's house was actually located in Beverly Hills, however.

Beverly Hills High School was used as inspiration for Bronson Alcott High, the fictional high school featured in the movie. Coincidentally, both Alicia Silverstone and Bronson Alcott (who played Travis in the film) both attended Beverly Hills High. Amy Heckerling, who wrote and directed *Clueless*, sat in on actual classes at Beverly Hills High to ensure the authenticity of the script. Herb Hall, who was a drama teacher at Beverly Hills High School, actually starred as the principal in *Clueless*.

The interior school scenes were filmed at Grant High School in Los Angeles. The exterior school scenes were filmed at Occidental College, which is also located in LA.

The Electric Fountain in Beverly Hills, Westside Pavilion Shopping Center in Los Angeles, and The Witch's House in Beverly Hills are also featured in the movie.

The movie brought about some new terminology that became popular for a time period during the '90s. Some of these terms included "betty," "baldwin," "as if," "whatever," "keeping it real," and "clueless."

This Celebrity Sex Icon Was Once the Second Choice for Queen at a California Festival

Norma Jean Mortensen "Marilyn Monroe" is one of the most well-known celebrity sex icons of all time. It's hard to imagine Marilyn Monroe being the second choice for anything, but she was.

Back in 1947, Los Angeles-born Norma Jean was crowned the first Artichoke Queen at the Artichoke Festival in Castroville, California. Norma was just 22 years old at the time, and she had not yet risen to fame.

Due to her lack of name recognition at the time, Norma wasn't the first pick for Artichoke Queen. However, the first choice wasn't available and Norma was.

Norma later went on to become "Marilyn Monroe," a stage name that she picked in collaboration with 20th Century Fox executive Ben Lyon. Lyon chose Marilyn because it reminded him of his sister and Norma chose her mother's maiden name, Monroe.

She starred in films like *Gentleman Prefer Blondes* and *How to Marry a Millionaire* and also became a singer and model. Additionally, Monroe had a widely publicized relationship with Joe DiMaggio, who was one of the most famous athletes at the time.

Castroville, which is known as the Artichoke Capital of the World, also went on to be successful. The town accounts for nearly 80% of artichoke production in the United States. Castroville's Artichoke Festival still runs today!

Lots of Songs Have Been Written About California

So many songs have been written about California that it would be nearly impossible to name them all. Some songs have been written about the people and places of California, while others have been written about Hollywood and a California state of mind.

Here are some of the most popular songs about California:

- "A Girl in California" by Merle Haggard
- "Beverly Hills" by Weezer
- "Blue Jay Way" by the Beatles
- "California Gurls" by Katy Perry featuring Snoop Dogg
- "California Love" by 2Pac featuring Dr. Dre
- "California Sun" by the Ramones
- "Cowboy" by Kid Rock
- "Free Fallin'" by Tom Petty
- "Hollywood" by Jay-Z featuring Beyoncé
- "I Left My Heart in San Francisco" by Tony Bennett
- "Malibu" by Miley Cyrus
- "Queen of California" by John Mayer
- "Santa Monica" by Everclear
- "Say Goodbye to Hollywood" by Billy Joel
- "Save Me, San Francisco" by Train
- "Surfin' U.S.A." by the Beach Boys
- "The Ghosts of Beverly Drive" by Death Cab for Cutie

- "Valley Girl" by Frank Zappa
- "We Built This City" by Starship
- "Welcome to the Jungle" by Guns N' Roses

These are just a few of the *many* songs about the Golden State!

Celebrity-Owned Restaurants in California

Thanks to Hollywood's presence in California, it's no surprise that a number of celebrities own restaurants in the Golden State. Here's a list of some of the restaurants owned by celebs throughout California:

- **Tagine:** Located in Beverly Hills, this Moroccan restaurant is co-owned by actor Ryan Gosling. Gosling and two of his chef friends opened the restaurant in LA because there was nothing else like it. The restaurant is known for menu items such as its black tiger shrimp, chicken bastilla, and lamb couscous.

- **Au Fudge:** Actress Jessica Biel may be best-known for her role as Mary in the '90s show *7th Heaven* and her marriage to former *NSYNC frontrunner Justin Timberlake, but she co-owns this restaurant located in Los Angeles. The restaurant has a Creative Space for kids, complete with an indoor treehouse and au pairs for hire, so parents can kick back and relax while they enjoy their meal. Some of the menu items include truffle grilled cheese, shrimp and grits, and Mrs. Timberlake's personal favorite: vegan Caesar salad.

- **Maria Maria:** With locations in Walnut Creek and Danville, Maria Maria is co-owned by Carlos Santana. Named after his song, the restaurant serves Mexican cuisine and offers live music.

- **Nobu:** With locations in both Malibu and West Hollywood, these restaurants are co-owned by Robert DeNiro. You'll find Japanese fusion food on the menu, such as Kaba ribeye and fresh sushi and sashimi. The restaurant is known for its homemade pistachio milk.

- **Ago:** Another one of Robert DeNiro's restaurants, this West Hollywood restaurant serves classic Italian food. DeNiro co-owns the restaurant with fellow actor, Christopher Walken, director Ridley Scott, and Miramax's executive producers Bob & Harvey Weinstein, and chef Agostino Sciandri (who the restaurant is named after). The famous restaurant was in an iconic lunch scene in the movie *Pulp Fiction*. Ago is well-known for its Tuscan-style flare and its extensive wine list.

- **Café Gratitude:** Located in San Diego's Little Italy, this plant-based restaurant is co-owned

Prior to her role in *Friends*, Jennifer Aniston starred in a series of failed TV shows. These included *Molloy, Ferris Bueller, The Edge*, and *Muddling Through*. After playing in four shows that all ended up being canceled, Aniston was feeling a little hopeless, to say the least.

Jennifer Aniston was at a gas station in Los Angeles when she approached Warren Littlefield, the former head of *NBC*. She was looking for words of encouragement and reassurance—which Littlefield gave her, but he gave her something else, too.

Warren Littlefield helped Aniston land her role in *Friends*.

While the show's producers originally wanted Aniston to audition for Monica Gellar, that fell through because Courteney Cox was already considered to be a good fit for the role. So instead, Jennifer landed the role of Rachel Green—the role that became Aniston's career breakthrough.

It's hard to imagine how different the cast of *Friends* would have been if Jennifer Aniston hadn't approached Warren Littlefield at that gas station.

Many Talk Shows are Filmed in California

If you've ever wanted to be a guest at a talk show, then California's one of the states you should be in! There are a number of talk shows that are filmed in

California. These include:

- *The Ellen DeGeneres Show*: You can hang out with Ellen at Warner Bros. Studios in Burbank, California. The show is recorded Monday through Thursday at 4 p.m.

- *Jimmy Kimmel Live!*: You can attend a live taping at El Captian Theater in Los Angeles Monday through Thursday at 4 p.m.

- *The Late Late Show*: Attend a live recording of James Cordon's show Monday through Thursday at 4 p.m. The Carpool Karaoke King's show is filmed at CBS Television City in Los Angeles.

- *Conan*: You can catch a live recording Conan O'Brien's talk show at Warner Bros. Studio at 3:30 p.m. Monday through Thursday.

- *Real Time with Bill Maher*: Attend a live taping of the political talk show. Located at CBS Television City in Los Angeles, the show is recorded on Fridays at 5:30 p.m. Audience members must be 16+ due to mature content.

Shirley Temple's Career Started Out in California, but it Wasn't Always Glamorous

Today she's remembered for her adorable curly hair and her roles in *Heidi*, *Curly Top*, *The Little Colonel*, and *Bright Eyes*. But did you know Hollywood's child starlet Shirley Temple got her start in California?

Shirley Temple was born in Santa Monica, California in 1928. When she was about three years old, her mother enrolled her in Ethel Meglin's Dance School in Hollywood. It was there that Temple was first noticed by a casting director, who gave Shirley her first contract.

It wasn't until Shirley Temple was five that she received a contract with Fox Films Corporation. Although this is where she got her big break and began to rise to fame, there was a lot of controversy over the abuse Shirley and other childhood stars endured from this production company. Children were forced to work under slave-like conditions.

Children were forced to rehearse for two weeks without pay and then were forced to film the movie within two days' time.

The production company had a punishment box, which contained an ice block. Children who "misbehaved" were forced into the box to cool off—a torture Shirley Temple was forced to endure. She was also forced to work after a painful operation on her eardrum and dance after a foot injury.

And then there was the issue of pay. At the time, Shirley Temple was only getting paid $150 a week and being forced to do commercials for free to underwrite the company's production costs. In 1934, Shirley's parents took Fox Film Corporation to court. The actress's income was increased to $1,000 per week with $15,000 for every movie she starred in. It's been estimated that this is the equivalent to $1.8 million today.

By 1939, Shirley Temple's acting career began to fail. She had been offered the role of Dorothy in *The Wizard of Oz*, but it ended up going to Judy Garland when Fox refused to loan her to MGM for the movie.

Fox soon realized that her childhood appeal had begun to fade and allowed her parents to buy her contract from them. After a series of flops at the box office, Temple retired from acting.

Temple went on to marry John Agar, with whom she had a child. Their marriage ended in a messy divorce due to his drinking problems and infidelity.

She later met and fell in love with Charles Alden Black, who had never seen one of her movies. Together, they had a son and daughter.

Later in life, Shirley Temple Black became heavily involved in California's Republican Party. She served as a U.S. Ambassador to Ghana and Czechoslovakia.

Temple passed away in 2014.

Tyra Banks Was Teased While Growing Up in

California

Tyra Banks was born in Inglewood, California and attended John Burroughs Middle School and Immaculate Heart High School in Los Angeles. It may come as a surprise to some since Banks' career is essentially built around her beauty, but the former model and creator of *America's Next Top Model* was teased in school.

According to various sources, Tyra has said she grew three inches and lost 30 pounds in three months when she was 11 years old. The former model said she looked frail and sick, even though she wasn't. Banks said she would "stuff food" down her throat in an effort to gain weight, but nothing helped. Her classmates made fun of her 98-pound, "too skinny" figure. They would call her names like "Giraffe" and "Lightbulb Head." Tyra felt insecure and alone, but she managed to rise above her peers' taunting thanks to her mentors and role models.

To help girls overcome the issues she experienced growing up, Tyra has started an organization called the TZONE Foundation in Los Angeles. The non-profit organization helps young girls build self-esteem, addresses gender stereotypes, encourages a love of one's body and beauty, and also encourages female entrepreneurship.

You Can Check Out the Tanner's House from

Full House

If you're a fan of *Full House* and the Netflix spin-off show *Fuller House*, then you already know the show is set in San Francisco. Did you know you can check out the house that's featured in the show?

The house featured in the show is Painted Ladies, a row of Victorian-style homes on Broderick Street, across from Alamo Square Park in San Francisco's Lower Pacific Heights. The exact address of the Tanner's house in *Full House* is 1709 Broderick Street.

There's good news and bad news.

First, the bad news. The house from *Full House* on Broderick Street was *only* used for the exterior shots in the opening credits of the show. There's been a lot of confusion about this issue amongst fans of the show. The interior of 1709 Broderick Street is *not* the same interior you see in the show. In fact, the house looks completely different on the inside!

The interior shots of the Tanner house were shot at Warner Bros. Studios in Los Angeles. Stage 24 at the Warner Bros. studio is currently being used to film *Fuller House* today.

Now, onto the good news. The *Full House* creator purchased the house at 1709 Broderick Street in 2016 for $4 million. He bought the house with intentions of restoring it to the way it looked in in 1987, which included painting the door red again. You can rest assured knowing that the Tanner's home has been restored to its former glory. Want proof? The same house is featured in the opening credits of *Fuller House*.

Even though you can't go inside, you can still take pictures of it — which more than 200 fans do when they stop by to check it out each day.

Maroon 5 Started Out as a Garage Band in California

Did you know the band Maroon 5 started out in California?

Maroon 5 frontrunner Adam Levine went to Brentwood School in Los Angeles. It's there that he met Jesse Carmichael, Mickey Madden, and Ryan Dusick. Together, they formed a garage band called Kara's Flowers. Their first show was at the nightclub Whisky a Go Go in West Hollywood.

An independent producer took notice of Kara's Flowers when they were performing on the beach in Maui, who they went on to record an 11-track album with. Kara's Flowers later scored a deal with Reprise Records and released their first album, *The Fourth World*, in 1997. Unfortunately, the album only sold 5,000 copies and Reprise dropped Kara's Flowers from the label.

After Kara's Flowers broke up, Adam Levine and Jesse

Carmichael went to Five Towns College in Long Island, New York. They later dropped out and reformed a band with Mickey Madden and Ryan Dusick. They decided to change their style and experimented with different music genres before deciding on groove-style music.

They were eventually signed to Octone Records and, at the advice of the label, gained a 5th member, James Valentine.

While he worked as a writer's assistant for the TV show *Judging Amy*, he wrote a bunch of songs about his ex-girlfriend, Jane Herman. These songs were the songs Maroon 5 recorded on their debut album, *Songs About Jane*. The album sold 10 million copies, and the band won a Grammy the following year for the song "This Love."

It's crazy to think that Maroon 5 wouldn't be the band they are today if those four guys hadn't met up at Brentwood High!

RANDOM FACTS

1. Tally's Electric Theater in Los Angeles was the first motion picture theater to open in the United States in 1902. The theater, which later came to be renamed The Lyric Theater, charged customers ten cents a ticket.

2. The band No Doubt is from Anaheim, California. The band launched female lead vocalist Gwen Stefani's music career, but there was originally supposed to be a male lead vocalist. John Spence, who formed the band with Gwen's brother Eric Stefani, was going to be the lead vocalist with Gwen as a backup. Spence committed suicide just days before No Doubt was going to be performing for record industry employees. The band moved forward with Gwen eventually taking the position of lead vocals. They gained a large following throughout California, playing with The Untouchables, Fishbone, and even the Red Hot Chili Peppers. Tony Ferguson of Interscope Records gave them a multi-album contract because he was impressed by their large fan following, who were frequently stage-diving at their shows.

3. Actress Blake Lively attended Burbank High School. She was senior class president, on the

cheerleading squad, and a member of the choir. Her breakthrough role, *The Sisterhood of the Traveling Pants*, was filmed during the summer between her junior and senior years.

4. George Lucas, the creator of *Star Wars*, is a California native. He was born in Modesto, California and currently resides in Marin County.

5. Independent films are popular in California. San Francisco hosts more than 50 film festivals every year. The city is home to everything from the Disposable Film Festival to the Greek Film Festival. The San Francisco International Film Festival is the oldest film festival in the United States.

6. You can see the house that was used for the exterior scenes in *Mrs. Doubtfire* starring Robin Williams at 2640 Steiner Street in San Francisco. The interior of the house was filmed at a warehouse in the Bay Area.

7. While he's most well-known for his poetry focusing on New England, Robert Frost was born in San Francisco.

8. Actress Cameron Diaz grew up in Long Beach, California. She went to Los Cerritos Elementary School and graduated from Long Beach Polytechnic High School, which she attended with another famous alumnus—rapper Snoop Dogg!

17. Actor Zac Efron is a California native. He went to Arroyo Grande High School and the Pacific Conversancy of the Performing Arts before landing his breakthrough role in Disney's *High School Musical*.

18. Jack London, the author of American classic novels *White Fang* and *Call of the Wild*, was born in San Francisco. He attended Oakland High School. Today, you can visit Jack London State Historic Park, which is made up of his home and Jack and his wife's graves.

19. Ellen DeGeneres hosted her high school reunion at her talk show. She flew 60 of the alumni from her graduating class to the studio where they celebrated their 30-year reunion.

20. One of the most well-known holiday songs was written in California. "Let it Snow" was written in Hollywood during a heatwave in July of 1945. The songs' writers, Sammy Cahn and Jule Styne, wrote it because they were dreaming about cooler temperatures.

Test Yourself – Questions and Answers

1. Which genre of music did *not* get its start in California?

   a. Surf music
   b. West Coast hip hop
   c. Jazz

2. Marilyn Monroe was crowned Queen at which festival?

   a. The Artichoke Festival
   b. The Almond Festival
   c. The Avocado Festival

3. Dr. Seuss got his inspiration for the Lorax tree from a type of tree that can be found at Scripps Park in La Jolla. The type of tree is a _____?

   a. Cherry Blossom Tree
   b. Cedar of Lebanon
   c. Monterrey Cypress Tree

4. Which celebrities attended high school together?

   a. Zac Efron and Blake Lively
   b. Cameron Diaz and Snoop Dogg
   c. Leonardo DiCaprio and Adam Levine

5. Which celebrity owns a restaurant named after one of his songs?

   a. Carlos Santana
   b. Adam Levine
   c. Jason Mraz

Answers

1. c.
2. a.
3. c.
4. b.
5. a.

CHAPTER THREE

FACTS ABOUT CALIFORNIA'S ATTRACTIONS

If you're thinking about planning a trip to the Golden State, there are a number of attractions you might want to check out while you're there. But how much do you really know about them? Do you know about one of Disneyland's most morbid early attractions? Do you know what the actual color of the Golden Gate Bridge is? (One hint: it's *not* gold!) Do you know about the famous tree that can be found in the state? Do you know how much it costs to get your name on the Hollywood Walk of Fame? Read on to find out the answers to these questions and other random facts about California's most famous attractions.

You Can See a Rainbow at Night at Yosemite National Park

If you've ever wanted to visit Yosemite National Park, then you probably know it has some really cool attractions. The park is so beautiful, that it even inspired the idea of national parks in general when Abraham Lincoln signed the Yosemite Land Grant back in 1864 to preserve the region—even though Yosemite National Park didn't actually come to be until 26 years after that, making it the third national park to be formed.

The park is home to over 400 species of animals and is most famous for Yosemite Falls, the tallest waterfalls in the entire world. Yosemite National Park is also known for its ancient giant sequoia trees and its granite rock formations, which cast a fire-like glow at sunset.

But did you know that Yosemite National Park is home to another beautiful natural phenomenon? It's one of the few places in the entire country where you can see a rainbow at night. Yosemite's nighttime rainbows, which are called lunar rainbows or moonbows, happen during the spring and early summer. Lunar rainbows occur when the sky is clear and the moon is full enough to cast its light over the waterfalls.

Having a Star on the Hollywood Walk of Fame Comes at a Hefty Price

Have you ever wondered how much one of those stars on the Hollywood Walk of Fame cost? They come with a whopping $40,000 price tag! Wondering who pays for them?

In order to receive a star on the Hollywood Walk of

Fame, one must be nominated first. Whoever fills out the application must list who will pay for the star. The star in question needs to agree to the nomination *and* they must attend the star's unveiling. The only celebrity who didn't attend the unveiling of her star was Barbra Streisand.

The first celebrity to receive a star on the Hollywood Walk of Fame was filmmaker Stanley Kramer in 1960. Since then, everyone from Mickey Mouse to Muhammad Ali has gone on to receive a star—or more than one star. Celebs can have stars in up to five categories, though the only celebrity who actually has five stars is Gene Autry.

The San Diego Zoo Was Home to the First Panda Cubs in America

Did you know that the San Diego Zoo is one of only four zoos in the entire United States that's home to giant pandas? In fact, the first two panda cubs to be born and survive until adulthood were born at the San Diego Zoo!

Bai Yun is a female panda who was loaned to the San Diego Zoo from China in an effort to help reduce the country's dwindling panda population. Part of the agreement was that all pandas Bai Yun delivered were to return to China after they reached their third birthdays.

In 1999, Bai Yun delivered her first panda cub at the San Diego Zoo. The baby panda was a female named Hua Mei, which translates to "China/United States." Hua Mei was conceived via artificial insemination. Her father was Shi Shi, a panda who had already been at the zoo.

In 2003, Bai Yun gave birth to another panda cub at the San Diego Zoo. The male cub was conceived naturally. He was named Mei Sheng, which means "born in the United States." His father was Gao Gao, another panda who was born in China and transported to the San Diego Zoo to father Bai Yun's offspring.

Since then, Bai Yun has given birth to four more cubs, all of which were conceived naturally. Even more, the zoo has been able to learn so much about giant pandas thanks to her.

Bai Yun can still be seen at the San Diego Zoo today, though she is now past the age of reproduction. Her last cub, Xiao Liwu, was born in 2012.

Disneyland's Opening Day Was a Disaster

Did you know that the opening day of Disneyland was actually a disaster?

Walt Disney may have spent *two decades* planning Disneyland, but he was anxious for the park to open just one year and one day after construction had started. The opening of the park was rushed, with painting and hammering going on until the park's opening was aired live on ABC—which 70 million Americans had tuned in to watch.

The live special, which was co-hosted by then-actor Ronald Reagan, gave Americans a look at the park. They got to see Magic Kingdom's four realms: Fantasyland, Tomorrowland, Adventureland, and Frontierland. What viewers didn't know was that behind the scenes, a total disaster was taking place.

Since visitors were only to be granted into the park on opening day via invitation-only, only 15,000 park visitors were expected to arrive. So, imagine the surprise when over 28,000 visitors made it through the gates, thanks to counterfeit tickets.

There were seven miles of traffic into the park, causing more traffic than ever on the Santa Ana Freeway. More lanes eventually needed to be added to keep traffic under control.

Visitors were disappointed to find that Tomorrowland wasn't yet ready. Some of the park's rides, such as Peter Pan and Dumbo the Flying Elephant, also weren't open.

The weeds around the Canal Boats of the Ride attraction hadn't been removed prior to opening day. Walt Disney had workers place exotic plant names in Latin next to them so that guests would think it was an arboretum.

Due to the 100-degree temperature, the asphalt on the Main Street, USA, melted into a sticky tar. The tar ended up getting stuck on women's high heels.

The plumbers Walt Disney hired had gone on strike, which meant the drinking fountains weren't working. The refreshment stands ran out of both food and beverages, causing many thirsty, sweaty people to leave the park.

Meanwhile, the Mark Twain's riverboat ride had been filled to capacity and caused water to wash over onto the deck.

Walt Disney promised that the park would be better equipped, noting that it might take a month before everything would be running smoothly.

Despite the park's disappointing opening day, people still wanted to go to Disneyland. Within seven weeks, the park saw more than one million visitors. By 2015, 750 million people had been to Disneyland.

And a Disneyland Ride Once Contained Some Creepy Props

Disneyland may boast itself as the "Happiest Place on Earth," but when one of Disneyland's most famous attractions opened back in 1967, it may have been one of the creepiest. Some of the ride's props were a little morbid, to say the least.

At the time of its opening, the Pirates of the Caribbean

ride contained skeletons. As in, *human* skeletons. The skeletons came from UCLA Medical Center. They were later returned and buried, though it's been rumored that one human skull is still part of the ride today.

You might also be surprised to learn that Walt Disney's original concept for the Pirates of Caribbean was nothing like the ride is today. He originally wanted it to be an exhibit people would walk through, rather than an actual ride. However, Walt decided a boat ride made more sense, so he decided to make the ride similar to It's a Small World. The Haunted Mansion was also originally planned as a walk-through attraction.

Balboa Park is Bigger Than Central Park

Central Park is the most well-known park in the country, but did you know Balboa Park in San Diego actually encompasses more space? Central Park is set on 842 acres of land, while Balboa Park is made up of 1,200 acres.

So, what exactly can you find at Balboa Park? The San Diego Zoo, for starters. The park is home to a carousel that was built in 1910, 15 museums, the Marie Hitchcock Puppet Theater, restaurants, and so much more. The first IMAX Dome Theater is also located in Balboa Park.

There's also Palm Canyon, where you'll find 450 palm trees and a historic path, which connects with a canyon and leads to Old Cactus Garden.

In addition to being larger than Central Park, many consider Balboa Park to be far more laid-back.

The Golden Gate Bridge Isn't Actually Gold

The Golden Gate Bridge is an American icon, partly due to its appearance in the opening credits of *Full House*. It might come as no surprise that the Golden Gate Bridge isn't actually gold. The bridge has a redder appearance. So, what is the color exactly?

The bridge's color is actually called "International Orange." For touch-ups, the bridge's paint is currently supplied by Sherwin-Williams. The shade wasn't originally considered for the bridge.

Carbon gray, aluminum, and black were all early color options. The U.S. Navy wanted the bridge to be painted black with yellow stripes to make it visible on foggy nights.

But the bridge's architect, Irving Morrow, didn't want any of those colors. He thought black and aluminum both didn't capture the essence of the bridge.

His inspiration came from the red primary steel beams at Eastern factories were coated in. He felt International Orange was unusual to find in engineering. The color made the Golden Gate Bridge stand out from the sky and water, and it's also visible in the fog.

You might be wondering why the bridge is called the Golden Gate Bridge when it's not even gold in color. The bridge is actually named after the Golden Gate Strait, which lays between the Pacific Ocean and the San Francisco Bay. The strait was named by John C. Fremont, an explorer who thought the strait was a natural beauty. Contrary to popular belief, the Golden Gate Strait was *not* named due to the California Gold Rush. Fremont named the Golden Gate Strait two years prior to the discovery of gold in California.

Knott's Berry Farm Claims to be America's First Theme Park

Knott's Berry Farm in Buena Park, California claims to be America's first theme park. While some historians disagree, there's no doubt that Knott's Berry Farm *does* have a long history.

The amusement park is on the site of a former berry farm, which was started by Walter Knott and his family back in 1920. The Knott family sold berries, jams, and pies from the farm's stand. In the 1930s, they began to serve fried chicken dinners from their tea room. Their fried chicken became a popular tourist attraction, so they began to build shops for restaurant goers to spend time in while they waited to be seated.

In the 1950s, Walter Knott opened a county fair on the property. It was then that the idea of a theme park came about.

By 1968, the Knott family was charging an admission of 25 cents. The then-famous Calico Log Ride was added to the park the following year.

The park added Camp Snoopy. Snoopy has been the park's mascot since 1983.

In the 1990s, the Knott family sold the theme park to the Cedar Fair Entertainment Company (who also own the famous theme park, Cedar Point in Ohio). The company added a few large roller coasters and other thrill rides.

In 2009, the park became Nickelodeon University— though many still call it Knott's Berry Farm.

As of 2015, Knott's Berry Farm became the 12th most visited theme park in the United States.

One of the Most Famous Trees in the World is Located in California

Did you know one of the world's famous trees can be found in California?

Located in Sequoia National Park, the General Sherman tree is the largest living tree in the entire world. The giant sequoia is also one of the oldest trees in the world. It's believed to be anywhere from 2,300 to 2,700 years old.

The General Sherman tree is, without a doubt, one of Sequoia National Park's biggest tourist attractions.

It may surprise you to learn that the General Sherman is *not* the tallest tree on earth. It's also not the widest. It's considered to be the biggest tree in the world based on its volume.

The tree is 275 feet tall and 25 feet in diameter and has an estimated bole volume of 52,513 cubic feet.

In 1978, a branch fell from the General Sherman that was 6 feet in diameter and 140 feet in length, which is larger than most of the trees throughout the United States.

SeaWorld Almost Didn't Happen

The first SeaWorld location opened in San Diego in 1964. The theme park was home to the very first Shamu, an orca whale who was captured by fishermen a year after the park opened. But did you know SeaWorld almost didn't happen at all?

The park was created by first UCLA graduates. Their original idea, however, was to open an underwater restaurant that had marine life shows. Instead, they decided to create a theme park that would compete with Marineland of the Pacific, a marine life-themed park that was popular at the time.

When SeaWorld opened in 1964, it was home to sea lions and dolphins. The TV show *Flipper* came out the same year, which sparked an interest in dolphins and helped SeaWorld get popular.

Death Valley is the Hottest, Driest Place in the USA

You've probably heard of Death Valley National Park, but did you know it's the hottest, driest place in the entire country?

Death Valley reaches temperatures higher than 120 degrees Fahrenheit in the summer. In addition, the region only sees about two inches of rain annually. In 1929, Death Valley didn't get any rain at all.

You might be surprised to learn that, in spite of the hot summer temperatures and lack of water, there is still life in the region. There are more than 1,000 plant species and more than 350 species of animals. Bighorn sheep and mountain lions are among the animals you might spot at Death Valley National Park.

If you want to visit Death Valley National Park without fighting the heat, then you might consider visiting in February when the average temperature is 72 degrees Fahrenheit. There's also an average .52 inches of rainfall in Death Valley during February.

The Hollywood Sign is Almost as Secure as

Fort Knox

Remember in the movie *Friends with Benefits* when Justin Timberlake and Mila Kunis climb on top of the Hollywood sign? The likelihood of that actually happening in real life is pretty slim, considering the Hollywood sign has nearly as much security as Fort Knox.

To prevent the sign from being vandalized, the Department of Homeland Security helped develop a security system that involves razor wire, infrared technology, motions sensors, alarms, and helicopter patrols. The sign is monitored 24 hours a day.

It might surprise you to learn that the Hollywood sign, which became a historical landmark in 1973, wasn't built due to Hollywood's movie industry. It was originally designed as a billboard to advertise the real estate development that H.J. Whitley was actively promoting at the time. The Hollywood Sign cost a lot of money to build. At the time, it cost $21,000 to build—which has been estimated to be worth more than $250,000 today.

There are Hundreds of Wineries in Napa Valley

Napa Valley is every wine lover's dream. You'll find about 450 wineries and about 815 brands of wine in the area. That's a lot of wine! How do you even know which ones to visit?

In 2017, Igor Sill ranked the 10 best wineries in Napa Valley as follows:

1. V. Sattui
2. Darioush Winery
3. Castello di Amorosa
4. Spottswoode
5. Inglenook Winery
6. Artesa Vineyards
7. Domaine Carneros
8. Luna Vineyards
9. Opus One
10. Stag's Leap Wine Cellars

Igor Sill created this list based on Yelp and TripAdvisor reviews, as well as his own experiences.

There's a Castle in California

If you want to see a castle, the Golden State might not be the first place that comes to mind. But California is home to a castle, which was built between the years of 1919 and 1947.

Hearst Castle was built as a home for William Randolph Hearst, who published the largest chain of newspapers in the late 19th Century.

William Randolph Hearst commissioned Julia

Morgan to design the castle, which cost $6.5 million to build over the course of 28 years.

The castle has 56 bedrooms, 61 bathrooms, indoor and outdoor gardens, a movie theater, an airfield, and 127 acres of gardens—just to name a few of its features. At one point, it housed the world's largest private zoo. There were once lions, tigers, grizzly bears, jaguars, cougars, monkeys, and even an elephant. Hearst sold his animals off when he had financial difficulties and after his death in 1951, most of the animals that remained were donated to local zoos. Today, there are still zebras that roam the land.

William Randolph Hearst entertained many famous people at his castle. Many of his parties were hosted by actress Marion Davies, who Hearst is believed to have had an affair with. Clark Gable, Cary Grant, and many other celebs attended his parties.

With its palm trees, the exterior of Hearst Castle wouldn't make you think it resembles that of a European castle, but quite the contrary. The interior of Hearst Castle bares such a close resemblance to European castles that the dining hall was used as a model for set designers for the dining hall of Hogwarts in the *Harry Potter* movies.

Hearst Castle is open to visitors today.

The Origins of Alcatraz Island's Name May

Surprise You

From 1934 to 1963, Alcatraz served as a "supermax" high-security prison on Alcatraz Island, which is located off the coast of San Francisco. It housed some of the most ruthless, hardened criminals during its time. Today, it's a popular historical attraction, likely due to its most famous inmate, Al Capone, AKA "Scarface."

It might surprise you to learn that Alcatraz Island's name has absolutely nothing to do with its prison. According to the Bureau of Prisons, the meaning of Alcatraz is "strange birds" or pelicans. The island was named in 1775 by Lt. Juan Manuel de Ayala, a Spanish explorer who was the first to map San Francisco Bay.

The name of the island is fitting. Alcatraz Island is known to be a great place to go birdwatching. Western Gulls are the most common bird that can be found on the island. You'll also find cormorants, snow egrets, black-crown night herons, and orange-footed pigeon guillemots.

From February to September, parts of Alcatraz Island are closed off to visitors to allow birds to nest.

RANDOM FACTS

1. California is home to more national parks than any other state in the country. Nine of the 59 national parks are located in the Golden State. These include Yosemite National Park, Sequoia National Park, Redwood National Park, Joshua Tree National Park, Kings Canyon National Park, Lassen Volcanic National Park, Channel Islands National Park, Pinnacles National Park, and Death Valley National Park.

2. Universal Studios Hollywood had more than 8 million visitors in 2016, making it the 15th most visited theme park in the world and the 9th in North America.

3. Channel Islands National Park is made up of five of the eight Channel Islands off California's coast. The largest island in the park is Santa Cruz Island, which is almost three times the size of Manhattan! Santa Catalina Island, generally known as Catalina Island, is another one of the Channel Islands. The island is most known for its beautiful beaches, Arabian horses, and golf carts, which are driven instead of cars due to the 20-year waiting list to own a car on the island. Buffalo Milk is a famous Catalina Island cocktail. It's made of crème de cacao, Kahlua, crème de Banana, and

vodka, which are poured over ice and topped with half-and-half, whipped cream, and nutmeg.

4. The California State Railroad Museum is located in Sacramento. The museum, which is the largest of its kind in the United States, contains 19 steam locomotives and exhibits honoring California's railroad legacy.

5. On Highway 99 in Madera County, there's a place where a palm tree and a pine tree can be found side-by-side. This location marks the border of Northern California and Southern California.

6. The Ronald Reagan Presidential Library and Museum is located in Simi Valley. When you're there, you can step aboard Air Force One, the plane which flew Ronald Reagan over 600,000 miles during his presidency.

7. At the top of Mount Diablo, you can see 40 out of the 58 counties in California. They are most visible on a clear day, especially after a winter storm.

8. Klamath Wildlife Refuge is home to the largest population of bald eagles in the entire country. Bald eagles can only be found there during winter, however.

9. Since 1937, more than 1,600 people have jumped to their deaths from the Golden Gate Bridge. About 26 people have survived the jump.

10. Caswell Memorial State Park is home to the riparian brush rabbit, which is one of the most endangered species of animals in the entire world. It's believed that only a handful of these rabbits remain in the wild.

11. Pier 39 gets 11 million visitors a year. The pier offers bayside views with sea lion sightings, shops, food, entertainment, and its popular 2-story carousel, which came from Italy in 2008.

12. The Golden Gate Park is rich in California history. It was home to 40,000 refugees following the 1906 San Francisco Earthquake, served the first fortune cookie in the United States, and was once home to Monarch the Grizzly. Another one of the coolest aspects of the park? Is Shakespeare Garden, which only features the plants and flowers William Shakespeare mentioned throughout his works.

13. Pacific Park on the Santa Monica Pier is the only amusement park in the entire world that has a solar-powered Ferris wheel!

14. Legoland in Carlsbad, California was the first Legoland to open in the United States. The first two parks were opened in Denmark and England. Out of the six Legoland theme parks, Legoland California is one of only three that offers a water park.

15. The Presidio of San Francisco was once a U.S.

Test Yourself – Questions and Answers

1. At which of California's national parks can you see a rainbow at night?

   a. Sequoia National Park
   b. Yosemite National Park
   c. Kings Canyon National Park

2. Which of Disneyland's early attractions contained real human skeletons from UCLA Medical Center?

   a. Pirates of the Caribbean
   b. The Haunted Mansion
   c. Mark Twain's river ride

3. The General Sherman Tree at Sequoia National Park is the largest tree in the world based on which of the following?

   a. Height
   b. Width
   c. Volume

4. The dining hall in Hogwarts in the *Harry Potter* movies was modeled after a dining hall at which of the following?

   a. Magic Kingdom
   b. Hearst Castle
   c. Alcatraz Federal Penitentiary

5. What is the meaning of "Alcatraz"?
   a. "strange birds"
   b. "beautiful birds"
   c. "seabirds"

Answers

1. b.
2. a.
3. c.
4. b.
5. a.

CHAPTER FOUR

CALIFORNIA'S INVENTIONS, IDEAS, AND MORE!

Have you ever considered what inventions have come out of California? A number of popular foods, products, and other inventions that you might use on a daily basis have originated in the Golden State. Do you know which popular snack food started out at a theme park? Do you know what frozen treat was invented by accident? Do you know which successful fast-food chain's first location opened in California? Read on to learn more about some of the things that started out in California.

Doritos

Today, they're one of America's favorite junk foods. Did you know that Doritos got their start in Anaheim? The popular snack food started out at Disneyland, to be specific!

Elmer Doolin, the co-founder of Frito-Lay, opened a restaurant that was located in Disneyland's Frontierland in 1955. Doolin's restaurant was called Casa de Fritos, which is called Rancho Del Zocalo today. The restaurant purchased its tortillas and taco shells from Alex Foods, a food distributor in Anaheim.

Doritos were inspired by Mexico's traditional totopo and chilaquiles. The restaurant began to cut up and fry extra tortilla shells, which it added seasonings to. Doolin originally had Alex Foods produce Doritos, but when the demand for the tortilla chips got too overwhelming, production was moved to the Frito-Lay plant in Tulsa.

The chips were sold under the name Doritos, which means "little golden things."

When Doritos hit the market in 1966, they were an instant success!

Barbie Dolls

If you loved playing with your Barbie dolls as a kid, you can thank Ruth Handler, who was a resident of Los Angeles when she invented the doll in the late 1950s.

Ruth Handler was watching her daughter Barbara play with paper dolls when she got the inspiration behind the dolls. She noticed that Barbara was assigning adult roles to her paper dolls, even though the dolls were infants.

Ruth Handler told her husband, Elliot Handler, about it. Elliot Handler co-owned a toy company called Mattel, which he ran out of an El Segundo garage at the time. Elliot loved the idea.

In 1956, Handler went to Europe with her children where she found an adult doll called Bild Lilli. The doll was based on a comic strip and kids loved dressing her in outfits. Ruth bought three of the dolls and brought them back to Los Angeles, where she redesigned them with the help of an engineer named Jack Ryan.

The doll, which Ruth decided to name Barbie after her daughter, first debuted at the American International Toy Store in 1959.

During the first year of production, 300,000 dolls were sold.

The company behind the Bild Lilli doll sued Mattel for copyright infringement in 1961. Mattel settled out of court and purchased the patent rights to the Bild-Lilli doll.

The same year, Mattel put out a male doll that would be Barbie's boyfriend Ken—who was named after the Handlers' son, Kenneth.

Rocky Road Ice Cream

Have you ever wondered who to credit for this delicious ice cream flavor? While it's unclear who actually invented Rocky Road ice cream, one thing is for sure: it *did* come from Oakland, California.

Fentons Creamery, a historic ice cream parlor, claims to be the original creator of the ice cream flavor. Fentons Creamery's candy maker George Farren allegedly created a rocky road-style candy bar, which he blended into chocolate ice cream. It's been said this inspired his friends to make their own version of the ice cream with one change: they used almonds in place of walnuts.

Those friends who were inspired by Farren's creation were none other than William Dreyer and Joseph Edy, who founded Dreyer's Ice Cream in Oakland back in 1929. The popular ice cream brand still markets the flavor as "The Original Rocky Road"—even though the original recipe probably wasn't theirs.

Regardless of who created it first, Dreyer and Edy are the ones who named the ice cream flavor. The ice cream was created during the Great Depression. Its name was intended to give people hope during the "rocky" times.

Fentons Creamery still serves Rocky Road ice cream today.

Blue Jeans

You can thank California for those blue jeans you're wearing! Levi Strauss, of the now famous Levi's jeans company, is credited with designing the first pair of blue jeans. You might be surprised to learn that the idea wasn't actually his.

Levi Strauss, a German immigrant, opened Levi Strauss & Co. in San Francisco. His brother owned a dry goods store in New York City and the San Francisco location was a second branch of the business.

One of his frequent customers was a tailor named Jacob Davis. In 1870, a woodcutter asked Davis to make him a pair of strong working pants. Davis added copper rivets to the button fly and pocket corners to give the pants extra reinforcement.

The pants Davis designed for the woodcutter were a huge hit and other customers wanted the same type of pants. Soon, there was so much demand for his invention that Davis couldn't keep up. He asked Levi Strauss for financial support. Strauss agreed since Davis was a regular customer. Together, Levi Strauss and Jacob Davis got a patent for the reinforced pants in 1873.

Although legend has it that Levi Strauss sold his first jeans to miners during the California Gold Rush, this is actually a myth. The first pair of Levi's wasn't created until the 1890s—about 31 years after the Gold Rush had ended. The rumor came about due to a false advertising campaign.

The first people to purchase blue jeans were factory workers. Over time, the trend caught on and the rest is history!

Popsicles

Did you know the Popsicle almost never came to be? It was invented in California by accident!

Back in 1905, an 11-year-old boy by the name of Frank Epperson accidentally left a fruit drink out overnight on the back porch of his home in Oakland. The temperature dropped to below freezing overnight. The following morning, Epperson found the frozen drink on the "stick," which inspired him to invent the fruit-flavored ice pop.

The idea stuck with Epperson over the years. He didn't go public with his invention until he was in his late 20s. In 1923, he sold the frozen treat, which came in seven flavors, at Neptune Beach amusement park. In 1924, he got a patent for his invention, which he originally named the "Epsicle Ice Pop". His children later convinced him to change its name to the Popsicle.

Martinis

Have you ever wondered where the martini came from? The famous cocktail got its start in California!

There has been some argument as to where, exactly, in California the now famous cocktail came from. Some argue that the cocktail came from Martinez, which is the city the cocktail is believed to have been named after. Others say the cocktail originated from San Francisco. In the early 1860s, the Occidental Hotel in

San Francisco served a drink called the "Martinez Cocktail." In both versions of the story, a California Gold Rush miner requested a drink and the bartender came up with the idea of the martini.

No matter where it got its start, the martini is one of the most well-known cocktails today. The original martini is made with gin and vermouth and garnished with either an olive or a lemon twist.

Since its invention, the martini has been offered in numerous flavor varieties, ranging from appletinis to chocolate martinis. There are even martini bars, which serve different types of martinis.

California Rolls

There has been some controversy over who actually invented the California roll.

It's been said that California rolls were invented by a Los Angeles sushi chef named Ichiro Mashita in the early 1970s. When he was working at the Tokyo Kaikan in LA, Mashita began to substitute avocado for toro (fatty tuna) and constructed the roll inside-out.

However, a chef named Ken Sousa at the Kin Jo sushi restaurant near Hollywood was the first to be formally credited with the California roll's invention. It was reported by the *Associated Press* in 1979 until it was later contested.

Regardless of who actually invented them, California

throughout the entire world. But did you know they pretty much originated from California?

While he didn't invent the first slot machine, a San Franciscan car mechanic named Charles Fey did a lot of fine touching. His redesigned concept is what brought the slot machine, which was originally called the "Liberty Bell" machine, to what it is today.

Fortune Cookies

While you might think fortune cookies came from China, you'd be wrong. Fortune cookies actually originated from California. While there are several theories on who actually came up with the idea, the most popular theory is that they were invented by a Japanese immigrant named Makoto Hagiwara. Hagiwara was a gardener, who was best-known for designing the Japanese Tea Garden in Golden Gate Park.

As the story goes, the Mayor of San Francisco fired Makoto Hagiwara from his gardening job. When the new Mayor hired him back, Hagiwara made him cookies with "thank you" notes inside. The concept of a cookie with a note inside became popular.

The Golden Gate Park is the first place to have ever served fortune cookies.

In 1973, the fortune cookie folding machine was invented in Oakland, California. This made it possible for Chinese fortune cookies to be mass produced for the first time.

Orange Julius

A trip to the mall in the 1990s or early 2000s wouldn't have been the same without Orange Julius. Did you know Orange Julius started out in California?

In 1929, Orange Julius was founded in Los Angeles. Julius Freed, an orange juice stand owner, was inspired by his friend who suffered from stomach problems. His friend couldn't drink orange juice because of the acidity. Freed wanted to make a drink everyone could enjoy.

To make orange juice stomach-friendly, Julius Freed mixed the juice with milk, sugar, egg, vanilla, and ice to create the Orange Julius.

The frothy drink was an instant hit with the customers. Almost overnight, Julius Freed's daily sales went from $20 a day to $100 a day.

Taylor Guitars

If you're a musician, then you've probably heard of Taylor Guitars. Did you know Taylor Guitars is headquartered in El Cajon, California?

In 1972, an 18-year-old named Bob Taylor got a job at American Dream, a guitar-making shop. When the owner decided to sell the guitar shop, Bob Taylor and his two co-workers—Kurt Lustig and Steve Schemmer—bought it.

They knew they needed to rename the shop and opted for Bob's last name, Taylor because it sounded most American. Bob Taylor also did most of the guitar-making, while Kurt Lustig handled the business aspects.

Taylor Guitars is known for producing some of the best-sounding guitars in the industry. The company also helped make the acoustic guitar what it is today.

Some of the most famous musicians who have played Taylor Guitars include Taylor Swift, Jewel, Prince, Dave Matthews, Jason Mraz, and Steven Curtis Chapman.

You can take a free, guided tour of the Taylor Guitars Factory in El Cajon at 1 p.m. Monday through Friday.

The Gap

The Gap, Inc. currently operates the Gap, Old Navy, Banana Republic, Weddington Way, Athleta, and Intermix. But did you know the very first Gap store started out in the Golden State?

Don Fisher was inspired by the success of The Tower of Shoes, which advertised that it had whatever brand, style or size of shoes a woman could want. Using the same business model, Don Fisher opened the store on Ocean Avenue in San Francisco in 1969. Doris Fisher, his wife, and co-founder of the Gap, gave the store its name.

Originally, the Gap only sold Levi's clothing. Don Fisher grouped the clothing by sizes. The store also guaranteed that it wouldn't go out of stock, as it replenished sold items from Levi's overnight warehouse. The store also offered LP records to attract a teenage audience.

Today, the Gap, Inc. is the largest specialty retailer in the United States and the 3rd largest international retailer. There are more than 2,000 locations of its stores in the USA and over 3,000 throughout the entire world.

The Hot Fudge Sundae

Although the origins of the hot fudge sundae have been contested, it's believed that the hot and cold treat got its start in Los Angeles.

Clarence Clifton Brown allegedly created the first hot fudge sundae in 1906 at C.C. Brown's, the ice cream shop he owned. Brown is said to have experimented with a few hot fudge recipes before getting it right.

He put it on the menu at C.C. Brown's when it was at its first location at 7th and Flower Downtown. The hot fudge sundae was an instant hit! In fact, the success of the hot fudge sundae brought in so many customers that Brown was able to move his ice cream parlor to Hollywood Boulevard. C.C. Brown's became a hotspot for both tourists and celebrities. The hot fudge sundae's popularity caught on and quickly became an American classic.

RANDOM FACTS

1. The Egg McMuffin was invented by Herb Peterson, who co-owned a McDonald's franchise in Santa Barbara, California. He first introduced the egg, cheese, and Canadian bacon sandwich, which is served on an English muffin, to his menu in 1972.

2. The jukebox got its start in California in 1889. The coin-operated phonograph, the invention that would later lead to the modern-day jukebox, started out at San Francisco's Palais Royale Saloon. Customers were charged a nickel a pop. In its first six months of use, the machine earned more than $1,000, which is estimated to be more than $25,000 in modern times.

3. The origins of the Shirley Temple drink have been disputed. One Hawaii resort takes credit for the virgin cocktail. However, most historians believe the drink, which was named after the child actress, was invented in California. Rumor has it that a bartender at Chasen's in Beverly Hills created the drink to serve the young actress a non-alcoholic beverage. The Shirley Temple drink is made of ginger ale, grenadine, and a maraschino cherry garnish.

4. The Cobb Salad got its start at the Hollywood

Brown Derby restaurant in the 1930s. The owner of the restaurant, Robert Howard Cobb, was working late one night when he decided to make himself a snack. He opted for a salad and leftover bacon, which he mixed together with some French dressing. He added the salad to the restaurant's menu not long after. The salad is made up of bacon, chicken, eggs, and avocados. Cobb Salad is still traditionally served with French dressing.

5. While sourdough bread wasn't actually invented in California, it did get its start in America in the Golden State. During the California Gold Rush, French bakers brought sourdough bread to Northern California. Boudin's has made sourdough bread since those times. Sourdough bread has been scientifically proven to taste better from San Francisco due to its tastier bacteria, which is used to achieve the sour flavor.

6. Pet rocks were created as a joke by Gary Dahl after listening to his friends complain about how much work their pets required. He told his friends rocks would be the perfect pets because they didn't require any care. Dahl created a humorous instructional manual for the pet rock, which was included when people purchased the product. In 1975, more than one million people bought Pet Rocks during the holiday season. Within one year, Gary Dahl became a millionaire on his invention.

7. The first working laser was invented by Theodore Harold Maiman in 1960. It was designed using a ruby crystal in his Malibu laboratory.

8. The first cable car in the world made its debut down Clay Street in August of 1873. Since then, they have been commonplace in San Francisco (though they were removed temporarily in the late 1940s, they were later brought back). While they're not the best method of transportation, they're still a pretty cool sight to see.

9. The modern hula hoop became popular after the plastic ring was sold by Wham-O Toy Company, which is based in Carson, California. The toy was inspired by Native American Hoop Dance. Four months after the toy was released in 1958, 25 million hula hoops were sold. Within two years, 100 million had been sold. The craze eventually died out in the United States in the 1980s, though it remained popular internationally.

10. The Mai Tai is made of rum, curacao, lime, and orgeat. The cocktail was created by Victor Bergeron, who owned Trader Vic's restaurant in Emeryville, California. Bergeron came up with the idea when his friends were visiting from Tahiti in 1944. Wondering how the drink got its name? As the story goes, Bergeron made the cocktail for them and one of his friends said, *"Maita'i roa ae!"*, which means "out of this world!"

11. The waterbed got its start in California. Charles Hall created the waterbed for his Master's Thesis project at San Francisco State University in 1968. Waterbeds were trendy in the 1970s when they were considered sexy.

12. The first wetsuit was invented in California back in 1952. It was designed by Hugh Bradner, a physicist at the University of California Berkeley. Sadly, his invention didn't take on right away. A lot of other brands began to develop wetsuits of their own. It wasn't until the 1990s that Brander actually got credit for being the wetsuit's original inventor.

13. The first videotape recorder was invented by a California native. Charles Ginsburg was working as an engineer at the AM-radio station KQW (today's KCBS). When he joined Ampex in 1951, he was behind the development of the world's first video tape recorder.

14. WD-40, which helps prevent and reduce rust, was invented in San Diego. It was created by Norm Larsen, who founded the Rocket Chemical Company. He also invented WE-40 as well.

15. The Gay Pride Flag, which is also often referred to as the Rainbow Flag or the LGBT Flag, was created in San Francisco by an artist named Gilbert Baker. Designed in 1978, the flag represents support and

unity for the LGBTQ community and is used during Pride month celebrations.

16. Fantasy football originated in California. It all happened back in 1962 when two Oakland Raiders employees, a sports reporter, and an *Oakland Tribune* sports editor took a three-week trip to the East Coast together with the Raiders. After they returned from the trip, they started the Greater Oakland Professional Pigskin Prognosticators League, which met weekly at King's X bar (today's Kona Club). This paved the way for fantasy football.

17. Skateboarding was invented back in the 1950s as an alternative to surfing. It was considered to be an ideal alternative when the waves in Southern California weren't good for surfing. Skateboarding has come a long way since it was first invented. The very first skateboard was a simple wooden board attached to disassembled roller blades. By the 1970s, the boards became more elaborate and an entire culture had been formed around skateboarding. In fact, skateboarding is going to be added as an Olympic sport in 2020.

18. The Nicotine Patch was invented by Murray Jarvik, a professor at UCLA, and one of his colleagues. Their research on the effects of nicotine absorption into the skin led them to develop the now-famous nicotine patch, which helps people

quit smoking. The nicotine patch was released in 1992.

19. The California burrito got its start at an unknown San Diego restaurant in the 1980s and has been a popular part of San Diego's culture ever since. The California burrito is generally made from chunks of carne asada meat and contains a surprising ingredient: French fries. It also generally includes pico de gallo, cilantro, sour cream, onion, and/or guacamole. With the combination of American and Mexican ingredients, the California burrito is considered a border fusion food.

20. The Jack in the Box fast-food chain got its start in San Diego when Robert O. Peterson opened it in 1951. It was the first fast food restaurant to make the drive-thru its primary focus, as well as the first to use a two-way intercom system for its drive-thru. Today, the chain has over 2,000 locations, which are located primarily on the West Coast and in select urban areas on the East Coast.

Test Yourself – Questions and Answers

1. Who was the Barbie doll named after?
   a. The inventor of the Barbie Doll
   b. The inventor's daughter
   c. A doll from Europe

2. Which cold treat was *not* invented in California?
   a. The hot fudge sundae
   b. The frozen margarita
   c. Popsicles

3. Who brought sourdough bread to the Golden State?
   a. French bakers
   b. Native Americans
   c. Latvian bakers

4. Fortune cookies were first served where?
   a. SeaWorld
   b. Universal Studios
   c. Golden Gate Park

5. Which popular snack food was first served at Disneyland?
   a. Marshmallow Peeps
   b. Doritos
   c. Fritos

Answers

1. b.
2. c.
3. a.
4. c.
5. b.

CHAPTER FIVE

CALIFORNIA'S UNSOLVED MYSTERIES, SUPERNATURAL, AND OTHER WEIRD FACTS

Do you know which unsolved mysteries have taken place in California? Due to Hollywood, it's no surprise that many of these unsolved mysteries involve celebrities. Have you heard about the creepy folklore and urban legends that haunt the Golden State? Some of the facts you read in this chapter may give you goosebumps. Others may surprise you. Some of them are just plain weird. To find out about some of the creepiest and most bizarre things that have happened in California, read on!

The Black Dahlia Murder Mystery

You've probably heard of the Black Dahlia by now. The case is one of the most famous unsolved murder cases in the history of the United States, as well as one of the oldest unsolved murder cases in Los Angeles County. But how much do you really know about it?

Twenty-two-year-old Elizabeth Short's body was found in Leimert Park in Los Angeles on January 15th, 1947. Her body, which was severely mutilated, was found severed in two pieces. The killer had also drained Short of all her blood before cleaning her body with gasoline to remove any fingerprints. Police were able to identify the victim based on her fingerprints, which matched fingerprints on a previous arrest record.

As the case began to unravel, the LAPD found that Short had last been seen six days before her murder. This led investigators to believe the victim had been kidnapped prior to being killed.

Elizabeth Short's boyfriend had dropped her off at a bar where she was supposed to meet her sister from Boston. One of the last people to have seen Elizabeth Short was a wealthy man named Mark Hansen, a movie theater and nightclub owner.

Newspapers often gave nicknames to murder victims during that time. There have been several theories about how Short came to be known as the Black Dahlia. There was a murder mystery film called *The Blue Dahlia*. Short also wore dahlias in her hair. It's been said that Short had already been given the nickname at the drug store she worked at prior to her murder.

Within the week following Short's murder, a person who claimed to be the killer called the editor of the *Los Angeles Examiner*, James Richardson. The alleged killer told Richardson he planned to turn himself in, but he wanted the police to pursue him further. The killer also told Richardson to expect some of Short's "souvenirs" in the mail.

Three days after the call was made, a manila envelope was discovered which contained newspaper clippings and Elizabeth Short's birth certificate, photographs, business cards, and an address book with the name Mark Hansen embossed in gold on the front. Like Short's body, the envelope had been cleaned with gasoline. While some fingerprints were still able to be lifted from the envelope, they were compromised on their way to the FBI and could not be used.

Due to the address book, Mark Hansen became a suspect in the investigation. Hansen knew Elizabeth Short and was able to confirm that a purse and shoe belonged to her. Ann Toth, who was Short's roommate, told investigators that Hansen had made sexual advances which Short had reject prior to her murder.

Mark Hansen was cleared as a suspect. However, author Piu Eatwell argues in her book about the case, *Black Dahlia, Red Rose*, that Hansen played a role in Short's death. She believes that the murder was committed by Hansen and a man named Leslie Duane Dillon, a mortician's assistant and bellhop. At one point, Dillon was a lead suspect in the investigation. Piu suggests that both suspects were let off the hook because LAPD Sergeant Finis Brown, who was one of the two cops who led the investigation, was a corrupt cop with ties to Hansen.

More than 150 suspects were interviewed, but no one has ever been arrested for the murder.

Over 500 people have confessed to the murder. Some people who have confessed to killing Short were not even born at the time of her death.

Conspiracy Theories Surround Marilyn Monroe's Death

Marilyn Monroe was found dead at her home on August 4th, 1962. The actress, who was found naked, had an empty bottle of pills nearby.

While Marilyn Monroe's death was believed to be a suicide, a lot of people aren't so sure. A lot of conspiracy theories came about after the actress's death. Nearly all of these theories revolve around Monroe's alleged involvement with the Kennedy family.

It was rumored that Marilyn Monroe was sleeping with John F. Kennedy. The rumor drew even further attention when Monroe famously sang "Happy Birthday" to the then President a few months before she was found dead. There was another rumor, too — that Marilyn Monroe was also having an affair with JFK's brother, then-Attorney General Robert "Bobby" Kennedy.

One popular theory is that Bobby Kennedy had Monroe murdered to cover up their affair. Another theory was that she had a diary with incriminating information about the family, which Bobby had her murdered for.

Other conspiracy theories were that the Mafia or the CIA had Monroe killed in order to hurt the Kennedys.

In a documentary called *Unacknowledged*, Dr. Steven Greer suggests another theory. He says that the United States government has been covering up extraterrestrial existence. Greer reveals a wiretap, which states that Marilyn Monroe knew about the government's cover-up and threatened to hold a press conference in which she would reveal all.

Is it possible that Marilyn Monroe was murdered due to her knowledge of aliens? Could this have been the same incriminating information she had about the Kennedy family?

In 2014, the diary of a late Hollywood detective named Fred Otash was found. Otash claimed that he heard Marilyn Monroe die. He claimed that Monroe argued with Kennedy before they had sex with her, causing her to scream. He said Bobby Kennedy used a pillow to muffle her cries so the neighbors wouldn't overhear. Bobby allegedly left immediately after that and Monroe's body was later found.

To date, many people still consider Marilyn Monroe's

death to be a mystery.

Natalie Wood's (Not So) Accidental Drowning

Natalie Wood was an actress who was known for her roles in the movies *Miracle of 34th Street*, *West Side Story*, and *Rebel Without a Cause*. She also dated famous celebrities, including Elvis Presley.

On November 28th,1981, while she was filming the movie *Brainstorm*, Natalie Wood and her husband Robert Wagner took a weekend boat trip to Catalina Island. They were on board a boat called the *Splendour* with Wood's *Brainstorm* co-star Christopher Walker and Dennis Davern, the captain of the boat.

The following morning, Natalie Wood's body was found dead one mile away from the boat. A dinghy was found on the beach.

Robert Wagner claimed that Wood wasn't in bed when he retired to his cabin.

Alcohol was found in Wood's bloodstream. Thomas Noguchi, the Los Angeles County coroner, believed she was drunk and slipped when trying to re-board the dinghy. Noguchi ruled her death an accidental drowning and hypothermia.

In 2011, Dennis Davern publicly stated that he lied during the investigation. Davern claimed that Wood was having an affair with Walker and Wagner, who was jealous and angry, had killed her.

Police have officially cleared Walker as a suspect, but Robert Wagner was named a person of interest in February 2018.

Californians Report Lots of Bigfoot Sightings

Did you know California is the 2nd state with the most reported Bigfoot sightings in the United States?

In fact, Bigfoot sightings are so commonplace in California that there's even a museum in Willow Creek, which is known as the Bigfoot Capital of the World. The Bigfoot Museum has the largest collection of sasquatch artifacts in the entire world. Most of the collection is from Bigfoot researcher Bob Titmus. Some of the artifacts you'll find include newspaper clippings, Bigfoot hair, and casts of Bigfoot footprints.

According to urban legends, Yosemite National Park was home to the world's very first Bigfoot. During one sighting at Yosemite, a camper was woken up by a strange sound. He ran out of his tent screaming, hoping to scare off whatever had woken him up in the first place. Instead, the camper found himself face-to-face with Bigfoot, who let out an even scarier scream before running off into the woods.

Redwood National and State Park is another place which is believed to possibly be where the first Bigfoot originated from. The very first widely publicized reported sighting of Bigfoot came from the park back in 1958.

The Patterson-Gimlin Film is the first recorded footage of what might be Bigfoot. The short film was shot alongside Bluff Creek near Orleans, California. The film was made by Roger Patterson and Bob Gimlin. Patterson maintained that the creature in the film was real up until his death in 1972. In 1999, however, Gimlin said that he believed it may have been a hoax set up by Patterson—one that Gimlin fell for himself.

A number of Bigfoot sightings have been reported at Mount Shasta. In 1962, one woman allegedly saw Bigfoot have a baby at Mount Shasta.

In 1993, a group of hikers reported seeing sasquatch across from Aloha Lake in Northern California. Since then, a number of Bigfoot sightings have been reported in the area.

The most recent famed Bigfoot sighting happened in 2017 when a woman named Claudia Ackley, who had been researching the urban legend for 20 years, took her two daughters hiking near Lake Arrowhead in the San Bernardino mountains. A few yards away and 30-feet up in a tree, Ackley spotted what she believed to be an 800-pound creature that looked like a hairy Neanderthal. When Ackley called authorities to report the Bigfoot sighting, they told her she had seen a bear and refused to offer assistance. What drew attention to Claudia Ackley's sighting was the lawsuit she filed a year after her report was made. The lawsuit is against the California Department of Fish and Wildlife for "dereliction of duty to protect Bigfoot" and infringing on her own constitutional rights.

The Death of Elisa Lam at the Cecil Hotel in Los Angeles

The story behind Elisa Lam's death at the Cecil Hotel in Los Angeles is so eerie that many believe it to be an urban legend, but it's not. It's all real—and it's all completely terrifying.

But before we talk about Elisa Lam's death, let's start at the beginning. The Cecil Hotel has a long history of murders and suicides. In fact, so many suicides took place at the hotel that it was once referred to as "The Suicide" instead of "The Cecil."

Attention was first drawn to the hotel when the Black Dahlia was said to have been spotted at the Cecil's Bar just days prior to her death.

In the early 1960s, one of the hotel's residents, "Pigeon Goldie" Osgood, was found dead in her room, which had been ransacked. Osgood had been raped, stabbed, and beaten. While a man named Jacques B. Ehlinger was charged with her murder, he was later cleared. Her death is still a mystery.

In the 1980s, the Cecil Hotel was said to have been where a serial killer named Richard Ramirez, who was nicknamed the "Night Stalker," had been staying for a few weeks. It's believed that Ramirez may have done some of his murders while he was staying at the Cecil.

Richard Ramirez isn't the only serial killer who stayed at the Cecil. In 1991, Austrian serial killer Jack Unterweger is believed to have stayed there to pay homage to Ramirez. During his stay at the Cecil, Unterweger strangled and killed at least three prostitutes. He was later convicted of the murders in Austria.

In 2013, the creepiest death took place at the Cecil Hotel, which had been renamed Stay on Main. After hotel guests began to complain that their water was a darker color, hotel maintenance discovered a young woman's nude body inside the water tank, located on the roof of the hotel. Her body had been decomposing in the tank for at least two weeks.

The body was identified as Elisa Lam, a young Canadian student who was traveling at the time. Lam had originally been sharing a hotel room before her roommates complained of her "odd behavior," and she got her own hotel room.

When police went through the hotel's security cameras on the day Lam is believed to have died, what they found was… well, bizarre and disturbing. In the video footage, Lam pressed the elevator buttons erratically and then looked out the elevator door when it opened as if someone had been following her. Once she exited the elevator, the doors opened and a closed a second time, but the person was never seen—leading some people to believe that Lam was being followed.

Although the Los Angeles County Coroner ruled Lam's death an accidental drowning, many have questioned how her body ended up in the water tank at all. There was no way to access the hotel roof, aside from the fire escape. Others have questioned if it was possible for her to have gotten into the water tank herself, which has led to speculation that someone may have murdered her and placed her body inside the tank. Could she have been trying to flee from the murderer when she was in the elevator?

Some believe that paranormal involvement may have played a role in Lam's death and that it could explain her erratic behavior in the hotel. Others have questioned if Lam, who suffered from bipolar disorder, may have been having a relapse at the time of her death. And still, others wondered if she may have been on ecstasy or another drug at the time of the video footage.

People have also pointed out that certain points of the viral video were slowed down. This has led to speculation that the video may have been tampered with before it was put on the internet.

One unusual theory is that Elisa Lam may have been

suffering from tuberculosis. Part of the logic behind this theory is the fact that the TB test is called LAM-ELISA.

People have compared the circumstances surrounding the death to the 2005 horror movie, *Dark Water*.

Things got even creepier when posts on Elisa Lam's blog continued to publish even after she had died. While it's most likely that Lam had pre-scheduled the blog posts, some believe it's her ghost. Lam's phone was never found, which also made people wonder if a possible murderer may have continued to post from the blog.

The mystery of Elisa Lam's death remains unsolved.

Alcatraz is One of the Most Haunted Spots in America

Did you know that Alcatraz Island is considered to be one of the most haunted places in the United States?

The theory of the island being haunted dates back to when the Native Americans visited Alcatraz Island before it was ever used for a prison. The Native Americans believed the island was home to "evil spirits." And they weren't the only ones who found the island to be… well, *eerie*. Author Mark Twain visited Alcatraz at one point and described it as "cold as winter, even in the summer months."

It's also been said that there are ghosts of prisoners

and prison guards who died at Alcatraz who haunt the former prison. One of the most scary places in the prison that's believed to be haunted is "the hole," which was once used for solitary confinement.

Rumor has it that a man was put in "the hole" in the 1940s. During the night, the man allegedly told the guards he was being tormented by a demon-like creature with glowing eyes who he believed was trying to kill him. The guards ignored the man's screams because they thought he was just trying to get out of the cell, but the following morning the man was found strangled to death. No one knows for sure how the man died, but people claim to hear the man's screams to this day.

The Zodiac Killer Once Killed in Northern California

You've probably heard of the Zodiac Killer, one of the most famous serial killers in American history. But you might not know that he killed his victims in northern California.

The killer's murder spree began in December 1968. Betty Lou Jansen and David Faraday were murdered in Benicia, California. They were both shot dead while sitting in their parked car. Without any witnesses or evidence, there wasn't much of an investigation.

In July 1969, Darlene Ferrin and Michael Mageau were

attacked in Vallejo, California. While Ferrin's gunshot wounds killed him, Mageau managed to survive the attack.

In August, three newspapers in San Francisco received letters from the killer. With the letter, the killer sent a cryptogram that he said would reveal his identity if it was solved. It was eventually solved, but it didn't reveal his identity.

On August 7th, 1969, the killer sent a letter in which he wrote his famous phrase— "This is The Zodiac speaking"—and it drew national attention and gave the killer his name.

In September of the same year, Cecilia Shepard was shot dead on the shore of Lake Berryessa, while her boyfriend Bryan Hartnell survived his wounds.

In October, Paul Lee Stine was shot to death in a taxi in San Francisco. It's believed that Stine was the final victim, though some investigators believed that the Zodiac Killer may have been responsible for up to 37 murders in total.

Following Stine's death, the Zodiac Killer sent a piece of Paul Stine's shirt with his letters to the newspapers. The killer also sent another cryptogram, which no one could solve, and a seven-page letter.

Throughout 1970, the newspapers received six more letters and greeting cards. The letters contained details about some of the things the Zodiac Killer had done in the past, as well as what he had planned for the future. Unfortunately, the letters didn't help police enough for them to come up with any potential leads or suspects.

The Zodiac Killer didn't give up, however. He continued to send letters for eight more years.

There was evidence that made investigators believe the Zodiac Killer may have also murdered victims in Lake Tahoe, Riverside, and Santa Barbara.

While the police have come up with several suspects over the years, there was never enough evidence for them to make an arrest.

In his book, *The Black Dahlia Avenger*, a retired police detective named Steve Hodel suggests that his own deceased father, a physician named George Hill Hodel, Jr., was the Zodiac Killer. Steve Hodel also believes his father was responsible for the Black Dahlia's murder.

The Zodiac Killer's letters stopped coming in 1978. While the case was marked inactive in 2004, it was re-opened at some point prior to 2007.

Dark Watchers May Haunt the Santa Lucia Mountains

The Dark Watchers are one of the most popular California urban legends. If you've never heard the story, it's a little creepy, to say the least.

The legend originates from the Chumash Indians, who lived in the region. The cave walls in the Santa Lucia Mountains were painted to show dark phantom-like shapes on the mountains looking down, as though they were watching.

In his story *Flight*, author John Steinbeck described the same figures as "dark forms against the sky."

A Monterey high school principal claimed to see the Dark Watchers.

Since then, there have been mixed reports about what the Dark Watchers look like. Some describe them as ghostly figures that wear dark capes and hats, while others report phantom-like figures like those described by the Chumash Indians. In every account, however, these figures are said to stay still as they watch from the mountaintop before vanishing into thin air.

The legend of the Dark Watchers has been around for centuries, so it seems safe to say that it will be around for years to come.

The Hollywood Sign is Believed to be Haunted

Did you know the Hollywood Sign is said to be haunted? According to urban legend, death is supposed to follow anyone who visits it alone.

So, what fueled this urban legend? A second urban legend. Almost every state has a legend about a Lady in White, and California is no exception. A Lady in White, with a skeletal face and eyes, is said to haunt the Hollywood Sign at night. It's believed that the Lady in White is late actress Peg Entwistle, who was allegedly driven to commit suicide from the top of the H after a bad review in 1932.

Entwistle isn't the only one who has died at the Hollywood Sign, however. The sign has been a popular suicide location. A man's decapitated head and body parts were also discovered near the sign.

If you're planning to try to get past the Hollywood Sign's security system, just make sure you don't go alone.

A Former Navy Pilot's Story About UFOs in California is Eerie

There have been numerous sightings of UFOs in California. In fact, based on information from the National UFO Reporting Center and the Mutual UFO Network, California is the state with the most UFO sightings in America. But one former Navy pilot's story is a little creepy, to say the least.

In 2017, former Navy commander David Fravor recounted his story of seeing UFOs off the coast of California in 2004. During his 15th year as a Navy pilot, Fravor was on a routine training mission when the squadron he was in charge of was ordered to go check out some strange unidentified flying objects that were being tracked for weeks. The objects were making a descent at 80,000 and 20,000 feet before disappearing.

According to the *Washington Post*, Fravor said what he found was a "white Tic-Tac, about the same size as a Hornet, 40-feet long with no wings" hanging above the water. Fravor said the UFO didn't create visible air turbulence the way helicopters do. He said the UFO mirrored pilots as they got closer before accelerating into thin air, moving faster than anything he had ever seen in his life.

When Fravor checked out the water, he didn't find anything besides blue water.

Fravor told *ABC News* that what he saw was "not from this world."

The Monster That Once Haunted Elizabeth Lake

Surely, you've heard of the Lochness Monster, but have you heard of the Elizabeth Lake Monster? In fact, there are several urban legends surrounding Elizabeth Lake, which is located near Lancaster in Los Angeles.

For starters, it's been said that Elizabeth Lake is a secret passage to Hell. The legend says that to get to the underworld, one must swim deep enough into the lake.

It has also been said that the lake was created by the devil himself as a home for one of his pets. In 1780, Spanish missionary Father Junipero Serra named the lake "La Laguna de Diablo," or Devil's Lake because people who lived nearby believed it contained the devil's pet. The lake was later renamed after a girl named Elizabeth Wingfield slipped and fell into the water. While the girl was okay, people began to call it Elizabeth's Lake as a joke and it caught on.

One of the first records of the monster came about in the 1830s, when a guy named Don Pedro Carrillo's ranch mysteriously burnt down. In 1855, people tried to settle in the area, but they were driven away by unnatural nighttime noises and other odd occurrences.

Not too long after, Don Chico Lopez, Chico Vasquez, and Don Guillermo Mentiroso gave the first description of the monster. They compared it to the size of a whale with huge bat-like wings. They claimed the monster roared and splashed water with either flippers or legs. Lopez also claimed that his livestock had been disappearing. Not convinced this wasn't a hoax? Lopez abandoned his ranch along the lake.

A rancher named Don Felipe Rivera reported seeing the lake monster in 1886. Not long after, another rancher named Miguel Leonis reported the loss of his livestock. He claimed to shoot the monster, only for the bullets to bounce off of it. The monster allegedly went back to the lake after Rivera's attack.

The good news is that this is the last report of the Elizabeth Lake Monster. In fact, it's believed that Don Felipe Rivera's attack on the monster drove it away from the lake.

Not long after it was believed to leave the area, there were reports of a similar lake monster in Tombstone, Arizona. There, the monster was seen flying in the area. A group of ranchers claimed to trap and kill the monster in the Huachuca Mountains. There is a photo from the 1890s of the ranchers holding what looks like a pterodactyl, which is what many believe the Elizabeth Lake Monster to have been.

The Most Haunted Ship in the USA is Docked in California

Did you know the most haunted ship in the United States is docked in the Golden State? The Queen Mary, which is larger in size than the Titanic, was used from 1936 to 1967. Since then, she has been docked in Long Beach, California.

So, why is the Queen Mary so haunted? It's been said that someone was murder inside one of the ship's engine rooms. Staff members have claimed to see apparitions in the room. Other allegedly haunted areas of the ship include the nursery and a few passenger cabins. Both staff and guests have reported hearing children laughing when no children were aboard the ship. People have also claimed to smell cigars, even though no one was smoking a cigar.

If you want to find out if the Queen Mary is haunted for yourself, you're in luck. The ship is a haunted attraction that's open to tourists. There are even haunted overnight stays aboard the ship, but beware: most of the guests end up having sleepless nights!

Writer Adam Mock wrote about his overnight experience for the site Crixeo. According to him, the entire ship is haunted, but most guests have more paranormal experiences on the B deck. Room B340 has even been closed to overnight visitors because so many guests were scared by poltergeist-like activity.

The Winchester Mystery House Might be Home to Spirits

Have you ever heard of the Winchester Mystery House? The house is the former residence of Sarah Winchester, widow of William Wirt Winchester, who founded the Winchester Repeating Arms Company. It's believed to be one of the most haunted houses in California.

After Sarah's infant daughter died and her husband died of tuberculosis, she was told by a medium in Boston that she needed to build a home in the West for herself and the spirits of people who had been killed by Winchester Rifles. In 1884, Sarah purchased a home in San Jose, California.

Sarah had builders work on the house day and night until it became a seven-story mansion. Since she didn't hire an architect, the house has a lot of strange architectural features, such as doors and staircases that lead nowhere. The mansion also contains secret passageways. Winchester was believed to have felt haunted by the spirits who had been killed by Winchester rifles and continued to have more work added to the house until she died.

Since 2017, people have been able to tour the Winchester Mystery House. You'll get a chance to see rooms that had never previously been open to the public, as well as rooms that hadn't been finished before Sarah Winchester's death in 1922. You can also participate in a séance in the house or spend the night if you're brave enough.

The Mystery of California's Gravity Hills

There are a number of "gravity hills" in California where a car will roll uphill when it's in neutral.

California's gravity hills can be found at the following locations:

- 1054 E. Loma Alta Drive in Altadena.
- Rohnert Park in Sonoma County. The gravity

hill starts at the "Gracias San Antonio" sign.

- 465 Mystery Spot Road in Santa Cruz.
- Rose Hills Memorial on Workman Mill Road in Whittier

Although scientists have come up with a number of possible theories for this crazy phenomenon, gravity hills have been the subject of urban legends.

The legend behind the gravity hill in Whittier is perhaps the creepiest. The gravity hill located at the cemetery used to be a sacred burial ground. It has been said that the spirits were awoken from their slumber by Satanic cult rituals and construction. To get revenge, they forcefully push vehicles down the hill. Some people have even claimed to hear strange knocking sounds on their cars when driving on the hill, which has said to be the spirits' hands.

The Skinwalkers of Joshua Tree National Park

In Native American culture, there's a legend known as "skinwalkers." Skinwalkers are said to be harmful witches or medicine men who have the ability to possess or turn themselves into an animal. It's believed that most skinwalkers take the form of a coyote or wolf. Skinwalkers are believed to exist in Joshua Tree National Park.

It has been said that skinwalkers terrorize and even *kill* campers at the park. The eerie part about it all is that people are often found dead at Joshua Tree National Park, while others have gone missing, never to be heard from again. Is it possible that skinwalkers could be possible for some of these deaths or disappearances?

RANDOM FACTS

1. Known for his role as Superman in the TV show *Adventures of Superman* in the 1950s, George Reeves died from a gunshot wound in 1959. While his death was ruled a suicide, it has been a controversial subject. His friends didn't believe he had committed suicide. Reeves was allegedly having an affair with MGM vice president Eddie Mannix's wife, Toni Mannix. It has been suggested that Eddie Mannix, who had mafia ties, might have had Reeves killed.

2. It's believed that Marilyn Monroe's ghost has been spotted throughout Hollywood. It's been said that her spirit appears near her tomb in the Westside Memorial Cemetery. There have also been sightings of Marilyn Monroe in full-length mirrors at the Roosevelt Hotel, one of the late actress's old favorite hangout spots.

3. People have claimed to see lost ships in California's Colorado Desert. While the Lost Ship of the Desert may sound like nothing more than a ridiculous urban legend to some since ships can't travel on land, it *may* be possible. There's a theory that former river ways may have led the ship to sink in the Salton Sea.

4. One of the most intense haunted houses in

America is located in San Diego. In fact, the Haunted Hotel has been ranked as the 2nd top haunted house in America. The haunted house gets about 24,000 visitors a year, and hardly any of them actually make it through the entire thing. You can expect to be pushed, grabbed, and exposed to numerous graphic displays. Do you dare to enter?

5. While California is best-known for Bigfoot, there's a scarier legendary monster who's believed to reside in Ventura County. The legend, which originates back to World War II, says the Billiwhack Dairy was home to some horrifying experiments. An OSS officer named August Rubel allegedly conducted the experiments in an attempt to make a "super-soldier" that would help win the war. Instead, Rubel created a half-goat/half-man monster, which he left behind while he went overseas to fight. The Billiwhack Monster is believed to haunt students who attend Santa Paula High School.

6. Turnbull Canyon was once known as "Hutukngna," a name it had been given by the Gabrielino Indian tribe meaning "the place of the Devil." The legend involves the region being haunted by spirits of Native Americans who were murdered for not converting to Catholicism. During the Great Depression, a Satanic cult was

said to hold their satanic rituals in Turnbull Canyon. They were known to sacrifice babies they bought and children from the local orphanages. One night, the cult mysteriously vanished. Hikers and locals began to report sightings of the children sacrificed, the spirits of the cult members in the form of hooded figures, and other paranormal occurrences. Since the reports began, other deaths have taken place in the area. A teenager was exploring the ruins of an old asylum in the canyon and ended up getting electrocuted. In 1978, 29 people died when a plane crashed in the canyon.

7. Highway 299 is said to be the most haunted highway in the United States. While the highway is believed to be haunted in more than one location, the stretch of highway near Old Shasta City is said to be the most haunted. Once a booming gold-mining town, Old Shasta City is now in ruins. Spirits are said to haunt the town's old courthouse and jail.

8. In 1922, silent film director William Desmond Taylor was found dead in his home. While he had been shot in the back, a supposed doctor had claimed he'd died of natural causes. While Taylor's butlers were considered suspects, the primary suspect in the case was then-young actress Mary Miles Minter's mother. Mary Miles Minter claimed in her unpublished autobiography that her mother,

who didn't approve of Mary's relationship with Taylor, was behind his death.

9. Bodie was once one of California's gold-mining towns. Today, it's a ghost town that's frequented by tourists. It's been said that the residents of Bodie were possessive about their town. But today, there's said to be a curse that goes like this: if you take anything from Bodie when you visit— even a rock—the spirits of the town residents will haunt you, *even if* you return whatever you've taken. There's an album at the park with letters from people who are suffering from the curse.

10. The disappearance of Anna Waters isn't only tragic. It's mysterious, too. Waters, who was just five years old at the time, disappeared from her family's backyard in San Mateo County. No one ever saw or heard from the girl, who went missing in 1973, again. Authorities believe she may have been kidnapped by a non-family member, but no one knows for sure.

11. The legendary "Dogman" is believed to be a type of werewolf. It's said to stand upright like a human, but it's generally covered in fur and has the head of a dog. There have been reports of the Dogman in Southern California. One sighting was reported in the foothills of the San Bernardino National Forest.

12. Rudolph Valentino was an actor who passed away at the ripe age of 31 due to complications from an ulcer. The late actor, who was a character in *American Horror Story: Hotel*, is said to haunt Studio Five at Paramount Studios.

13. The Battery Point Lighthouse, which is one of the oldest lighthouses in California, has been said to be haunted for more than 100 years. Paranormal researchers believe the lighthouse to be haunted by the ghosts of a child and two adults. Museum visitors have been said to feel their shoulders being touched or sense a presence, see a rocking chair move back and forth when no one is sitting on it, and hear the sound of footsteps climbing the lighthouse stairway when no one is there.

14. The cemetery that lays adjacent to Mission San Jose, Fremont has been said to be haunted. People have reported the sound of cries and cold spots. There have also been reported sightings of what are believed to be Native American spirits. People have claimed to see Native Americans cross the street and then disappear once they enter the courtyard of the Mission.

15. Located in Grass Valley, the Holbrook Hotel opened in 1852 during the California Gold Rush. Today, it's said to be haunted by multiple ghosts, including the Suicide Gambler. Rumor has it that he was found in a pool of blood after slitting his

own throat.

16. The mystery of James Gilmore Jr.'s death is an unsettling one. Known as a high school bully and a member of a motorcycle gang, 14-year-old James Gilmore Jr. disappeared after leaving his family's home in Baldwin Park in 1962. His remains were found 20 years later in a shallow grave underneath the family's house. The circumstances surrounding his death remain a mystery.

17. The Colorado Street Bridge Curse is one of Pasadena's eeriest urban legends. As the story goes, a construction worker fell off the bridge back when it was being built. His body was allegedly encased in concrete and his remains were never found. It's been said that the man's spirit haunts the bridge, which is what has driven many people to commit suicide or attempt to commit suicide by jumping off the bridge.

18. Stow Lake in San Francisco is believed to be home to a ghost known as the "Ghost of Stow Lake." As the story goes, two women were sitting on a park bench when one of the women didn't notice that her baby's stroller had rolled away. The woman allegedly looked everywhere in the park for the baby, asking park goers, "Have you seen my baby?" The woman searched the lake for her baby and she never resurfaced. Today, there's a statue at the park in her honor. Her spirit is believed to

haunt Stow Lake at night. She's been said to ask people if they've seen her baby. Depending on how you answer her, she might haunt or kill you.

19. Thelma Todd was an actress in the late 1920s/early 1930s who was known as "Hot Toddy." Her dead body was found inside a garage, but the circumstances surrounding her death didn't exactly line up. Her nose was broken and her blood alcohol level was so high that people didn't think she would have been able to climb the stairs to the garage. Rumor has it that Ronald West, Todd's boyfriend at the time of her death, confessed on his deathbed to accidentally locking the actress in the garage. However, others have questioned if Thelma Todd may have been killed by her ex-husband or gang leader Charles "Lucky" Luciano, who she'd allegedly gotten into confrontations with not long before she died.

20. Since people began hiking Mount Shasta, there have been reports of "little people." They have been said to live in caves, which leads many to believe they could be fairies. These people come out and are said to act like gremlins who try to sabotage people hiking the mountain. To try to keep them happy, some hikers leave out peace offerings in the form of food.

Test Yourself – Questions and Answers

1. Which of the following is recognized as one of the most haunted places in America?
   a. Catalina Island
   b. Alcatraz
   c. San Francisco

2. Skinwalkers are said to exist at which of California's national parks?
   a. Yosemite National Park
   b. Sequoia National Park
   c. Joshua Tree National Park

3. The most haunted highway in California is:
   a. Route 66
   b. Highway 299
   c. State Route 1

4. What is the name of America's most haunted ship, which is docked in Long Beach?
   a. The Titanic
   b. The Mary Celeste
   c. The Queen Mary

5. The Black Dahlia's real name was:
   a. Elizabeth Short
   b. Marilyn Monroe
   c. Dahlia Black

Answers

1. b.
2. c.
3. b.
4. c.
5. a.

CHAPTER FIVE

CALIFORNIA'S SPORTS

Whether or not you're a sports fanatic, California has a rich sports history. For example, do you know which international sporting event has been held in the Golden State? Do you know which famous athletes got their start in California? To find out the answers to these questions and other cool facts about California's sports, read on!

California is the Only State That's Hosted Both the Summer *and* the Winter Olympics

Not only does California hold the record of being the only state to host both the Summer and Winter Olympics, but it's also hosted the Olympics *three times*!

The Summer Olympics were held in Los Angeles in both 1932 and 1984, while Squaw Valley hosted the Winter Olympics in 1960. Here are some of the American highlights from each of these three games.

1932 Summer Olympics:

- The Victory Podium made its debut.

- Babe Didrikson won two gold medals in javelin and hurdles.

140

- Helene Madison won three swimming gold medals.

- Los Angeles' Tenth Street's name was changed to Olympic Boulevard in honor of the Olympics' 10th anniversary.

1984 Summer Olympics:

- The Olympic rings were formed by the United States Army for the opening ceremony.

- The U.S.A. set the record for the highest number of gold medals won in a single Summer Olympics. A total of 83 gold medals were won that year.

- Track and field athlete Carl Lewis won four gold medals.

- Edwin Moses won a gold medal for the first time in 8 years.

1960 Winter Olympics:

- *CBS* bought exclusive rights to broadcast the Olympics.

- Walt Disney produced the opening and closing ceremonies.

- The United States won an unexpected gold medal in ice hockey.

- David Jenkins won the Olympic gold medal in men's figure skating, while Carol Heiss took home the gold in women's figure skating.

- Women competed in speed skating for the first time.

Today, the Olympic Museum in Squaw Valley honors the legacy of the 1960 Winter Olympics games. At the museum, you can expect to find athlete memorabilia, authentic American Olympics uniforms, a hockey stick and puck from the 1960 games, and other artifacts.

There are More Professional Sports Teams in California Than Any Other State

Did you know the Golden State is home to more professional sports teams than any other state in the country?

California professional sports teams include:

Major League Baseball:

1. Los Angeles Angels
2. Los Angeles Dodgers
3. San Diego Padres
4. Oakland Athletics
5. San Francisco Giants

National Football League:

1. San Francisco 49ers

2. Los Angeles Chargers

3. Los Angeles Rams

4. Oakland Raiders

National Basketball Association:

1. Los Angeles Clippers

2. Los Angeles Lakers

3. Golden State Warriors

4. Sacramento Kings

National Hockey League:

1. Anaheim Ducks

2. Los Angeles Kings

3. San Jose Sharks

Major League Soccer:

1. LA Galaxy

2. Los Angeles FC

3. San Jose Earthquakes

Women's National Basketball Association:

1. Los Angeles Sparks

The Oldest College Bowl Game Takes Place in California Every Year

The country's oldest college football bowl game is held in Pasadena, California. Every January, the game is held at the Rose Bowl—the oldest stadium and one of only four stadiums that's recognized as a National Historic Landmark in the United States!

The first Rose Bowl game was played in 1902. Early on, the game was held at Tournament Park. At that point, the game was called the Tournament East-West Football Game.

It wasn't until 1922 that the Rose Bowl stadium was built. The following year, the game was held there for the very first time. The game has been held at the stadium ever since, except for in 1942 when the game was moved to Duke University following the attack on Pearl Harbor.

Today, the Rose Bowl is a highly anticipated televised event among college football fans. The game was televised for the very first time in 1952.

A number of well-known professional football players have won the MVP award for the Rose Bowl. Some of these include O.J. Simpson, Ernie Nevers, Charley Trippi, Jim Plunkett, Sam Cunningham, Mark Sanchez, Jack Del Rio, and Andy Dalton.

Tiger Woods's Career Started at a Navy Golf Course in California

Did you know that the golf legend Tiger Woods is from California?

Tiger, whose real name is Eldrick Tont Woods, was born in Cypress, California. The name Tiger came about to honor his father's friend, who was also nicknamed Tiger.

Tiger Woods grew up in Orange County where he began to play golf at the age of two. Tiger's father, Earl Woods, is the one who introduced him to golf. Earl was in the military and was given privileges to play golf at the Navy golf course in Los Alamitos. Tiger also played golf at several courses throughout Long Beach.

Tiger Woods began to receive recognition at a very young age. Most people considered him a child golf prodigy. When Woods was just three years old, he putted against Bob Hope on *The Mike Douglas Show*. The same year, Woods shot a 48 over nine holes. At five years old, he made it into an issue of *Golf Digest* and was also featured on ABC's *That's Incredible!*

Tiger Woods won the Junior World Golf Championships a total of six times, which included four consecutive wins. The first time he won, he was only eight years old and competed in the 9-10 boys event.

While Tiger Woods was attending Western High School in Anaheim, he became the youngest U.S. Junior Amateur Champion. He held this record until 2010 when it was broken by Jim Liu. Woods played on his high school's golf team and was recruited to

Stanford University thanks to his achievements in the sport.

By the age of 20, Tiger Woods became a professional golfer and signed a deal with Nike, Inc.

Major Surfing Competitions are Held in California

When you think of surfing competitions, Hawaii might be the first state that comes to mind. But did you know that some major surfing competitions are held in California?

The biggest surfing competition that's held in the state is the U.S. Open of Surfing, which is held every year in Huntington Beach. The week-long event is the largest surfing competition in the entire world. The first U.S. Open in Surfing was held in 1959. Today, it adds $21.5 million to Orange County's economy and is attended by nearly half a million people every year. During the event, people are also added to the Surfers' Walk of Fame and the Surfers' Hall of Fame, which are both located across from the Huntington Beach Pier.

Titans of the Mavericks is another major surfing competition that's held in the Golden State. Held in Mavericks, California, it's a big wave surfing competition. Thirty of the best international surfers compete each year. Waves can reach up to 60 feet in height. The first competition was held in 1999.

California is Home to the Salinas Rodeo

The California Rodeo Salinas is the largest rodeo in the Golden State. It's considered to be one of the top 20 rodeo events in the United States, as well as one of the 10 rodeos that are aired on ESPN, FOX Sports, and other television networks every year.

The Salinas Rodeo got its start back in 1910. At that time, it was a Wild West Show and took place on the old race track ground. Today, it's held at the Salinas Sports Complex—a 17,000-seat stadium.

The rodeo, which takes place every year, is a four-day event. The top cowboys and cowgirls from the Professional Rodeo Cowboys Association compete at the event for both money and the gold and silver belt buckles that are given out as prizes each year. Some of the events that are held at the rodeo each year include bull riding, steer wrestling, team roping, and more.

The California Rodeo Salinas also gives back approximately $400,000 each year to local non-profits.

One California NFL Team Was Named After the Gold Rush

Did you know the San Francisco 49ers got their name because of the California Gold Rush?

During the California Gold Rush, gold miners were called "49ers." The reason for this was because they migrated to California in search of gold in 1849.

The team's franchise is actually legally registered as the "San Francisco Forty Niners."

The team's name relating to California doesn't end there. The mascot for the San Francisco 49ers is also named thanks to the city. The mascot is a gold miner named Sourdough Sam. Sourdough, of course, came from San Francisco's reputation and history of being the best place to get sourdough bread.

A New York Yankees Legend is From California

Famous New York Yankees player Joe DiMaggio's baseball career got started in California! DiMaggio, who was born in Martinez, California, got his start as an athlete thanks to his older brother, Vince DiMaggio.

Vince was playing as a shortstop for the San Francisco Seals of the Pacific Coast League, a former minor league baseball team when he asked his manager to let Joe fill in for him in 1932.

Joe DiMaggio, who was named the Pacific Coast League's MVP, had his contract purchased by the New York Yankees for $55,000.

DiMaggio is considered one of the Yankees most legendary players. He played in nine World Series championships, in which the Yankees won.

Joe DiMaggio was given his nickname "The Yankees

Clipper" in 1939 by Arch McDonald, the New York Yankees stadium announcer. McDonald compared DiMaggio's speed and range to the Pan American outline, which was a novel invention at the time.

DiMaggio was also well-known for his widely publicized marriage to Marilyn Monroe.

And So is a Boston Red Sox Legend!

Did you know that the late Red Sox legend Ted Williams was born in San Diego, California?

When Ted Williams was growing up in the North Park neighborhood of San Diego, his uncle Saul Venzor taught him how to throw a baseball. Throughout his career as a semi-professional baseball player, Venzor had pitched against Babe Ruth, Joe Gordon, and Lou Gehrig.

Williams attended Herbert Hoover High School in San Diego. He was the star of the school's baseball team, for which he was the pitcher.

Ted Williams was offered to join the New York Yankees and the St. Louis Cardinals while he was still in high school! His mom thought he was too young, however, so Williams played for the San Diego Padres with the local minor league instead.

He later went on to join the Boston Red Sox, who traded Ben Chapman to the Cleveland Indians just so they could make room for Ted Williams.

To this day, Ted Williams is still considered to have been the best hitter of all time.

These Famous Tennis Sisters are From California

Famous tennis-playing sisters Serena and Venus Williams are from California! Both sisters were born in Lynwood, California. They were raised in Compton, California.

Serena Williams began playing tennis in Compton when she was just three years old! By the time Venus was seven and Serena was eight, their talents on the tennis court began to gain recognition.

When the girls were 10 and 11, their parents moved the family from Compton to West Palm Beach, Florida so they could receive better tennis training.

Today, Venus Williams is a four-time Olympic gold medalist and one-time silver Olympic medalist. She ties with Kathleen McKane Godfree for the most tennis medals to ever be won by a tennis player.

Serena Williams has won four Olympic gold medals.

O.J. Simpson Had a Troubled Youth While Growing Up in California

Today, he's most well-known for the controversial murder of his wife. But did you know that former football player O.J. had a troubled youth growing up in California?

Orenthal James "O.J." Simpson was born in San Francisco. He was raised in the housing projects of the Potrero Hill neighborhood of San Francisco.

O.J. Simpson attended Galileo High School in San Francisco. During his teens, he got involved in a street gang called the Persian Warriors. He spent some time in a juvenile detention center called the San Francisco Youth Guidance Center.

After he was arrested for the third time, O.J. Simpson met former MLB player Willie Mays. Mays encouraged Simpson to reform his life and stay out of trouble. This encouraged O.J. Simpson to play for the high school football team, the Galileo Lions.

Simpson later went on to play college football, even winning the Heisman Trophy. He later went on to play for the Buffalo Bills and then the San Francisco 49ers. While his wife's murder remains a highly controversial topic, especially after O. J. Simpson's book *If I Did It*, many still consider him to have been one of the most successful football players of all time.

The First African-American to Play Major League Baseball Grew Up in California

Jackie Robinson was the first African-American to play for the MLB. Did you know he grew up in California?

Although Jackie Robinson was born in Cairo, Georgia, his mother moved the family to California after his father abandoned them when Jackie was just one year old. Robinson lived with his family at 121 Pepper Street in Pasadena.

Robinson grew up poor in an otherwise wealthy community, which led him to join a neighborhood gang. However, his friend encouraged him to leave.

Robinson attended Washington Junior High School and John Muir High School (Muir Tech) in Pasadena. When he attended Muir Tech, Robinson played varsity baseball where he played in the catcher and shortstop positions. He also played football, track, basketball, and tennis.

In 1936, Jackie Robinson earned a spot on the Pomona baseball tournament all-star team. The team also included Ted Williams and Bob Lemon. Robinson, Williams, and Lemon were all later inducted into the Baseball Hall of Fame.

After he graduated from Muir Tech, Robinson went to Pasadena Junior College where he continued to play in baseball, basketball, track, and tennis. He was the shortstop and leadoff hitter for the team.

He continued in all four sports when he later attended UCLA, becoming the first athlete from the school to win varsity letters in baseball, basketball, football, and track.

After Robinson was drafted and returned from the military, he began a career in professional baseball. He started out playing in the Negro leagues before playing in minor leagues.

History was made when Jackie Robinson signed a contract with the Brooklyn Dodgers, which marked the end of segregation in professional baseball. Robinson had a major influence on the Civil Rights Movement.

The First Owner of the Los Angeles Angels May Surprise You

Did you know that the Los Angeles Angels' first owner was a celebrity? It was none other than the legendary Gene Autry!

The Los Angeles Angels weren't the first team Gene Autry owned, either. Autry, who had once turned down playing in the minor leagues himself, owned the minor league team, the Hollywood Stars in the 1950s.

When the MLB announced that it wanted to start a team in Los Angeles, Gene Autry wanted the broadcast rights to the games. Major League Baseball executives found the plan so impressive that they convinced Autry to become the team's franchise owner.

The Los Angeles Angels, which got their start in 1961, were named after a minor league of the same name of the former Pacific Coast League. Gene Autry paid $350,000 for the right to name the team the Angels! The Dodgers were actually going to be called the Los Angeles Angels first, but Autry bought the rights from Walter O'Malley, the former owner of the Dodgers.

The Los Angeles Angels' team name has changed quite a few times. When the team moved to Anaheim in 1966, they were renamed the California Angels. In 1997 through 2005, they were the Anaheim Angels. Then they became the Los Angeles Angels of Anaheim. They became the Los Angeles Angels again in 2016, which is what they are currently known as. Time will tell if the team changes their name again in the future!

Bethany Hamilton is Honored at the California Surf Museum

Famous professional surfer Bethany Hamilton rose to fame after she survived a shark attack. Hamilton lost her arm during the attack but with hard work and determination, she was able to return to professional surfing. The movie *Soul Surfer*, which is based on Hamilton's book of the same name, made her a household name.

Did you know you can see artifacts from Hamilton's attack at the California Surf Museum in Oceanside, California? At the museum, you will find Hamilton's shark-bitten surfboard and the bathing suit she wore during the attack.

Fun fact: Bethany Hamilton came in 5th place at the U.S. Open of Surfing in 2008!

A Famous Figure Skater is From the Golden State

Michelle Kwan may be one of the most recognizable names when it comes to female figure skaters. Did you know the former figure skater is from California?

Kwan was born in Torrance, California. Her parents had immigrated to the state from Hong Kong.

When Michelle Kwan was just five years old, she began to develop an interest in ice skating, a sport in which both of her older siblings participated in. Her brother, Ron, was an ice hockey player, while her sister, Karen, was also a figure skater. When Michelle was eight years old, both she and Karen began to receive serious coaching in figure skating. They trained for 3-4 hours daily, before and after school.

The cost of training took a financial toll on the Kwan family, however, and they were unable to afford a coach when Michelle reached 10. Fortunately, a fellow member of the Los Angeles Figure Skating Club offered the family financial assistance. The girls trained at the Ice Castle International Training Center, which is located in Lake Arrowhead, California.

Michelle Kwan attended Soleado Elementary School

in Palos Verdes, California prior to her homeschooling, which began when she was in the 8th grade. Kwan attended UCLA for one year before transferring to the University of Denver.

By 2003, Kwan won two Olympic gold medals and was a five-time World champion in figure skating. Kwan and Carol Heiss (who has also won five World Championship titles) both hold the American record for the highest number of World titles. She also holds nine world medals, which is the highest number of any American figure skater. And to think her success all started out in California!

RANDOM FACTS

1. NASCAR legend Jeff Gordon was born in Vallejo, California. The first racetrack Gordon ever raced on is the Roy Hayer Memorial Race Track in Rio Lindo, California when he was five years old.

2. The San Francisco 49ers were the city's first professional sports team. The team entered the NFL in 1950.

3. Downhill ski racing got its start in California! The oldest downhill ski racing on record took place in Plumas County in 1860. The Plumas-Eureka Ski Bowl is a yearly competition held in the region.

4. New England Patriots quarterback Tom Brady is from San Mateo, California. Brady went to Junipero Serra High School in San Mateo where he was first a backup quarterback on the junior varsity team. As a kid, Tom Brady regularly went to San Francisco 49ers games and was a big fan of Joe Montana, who Brady has said was his role model.

5. The Los Angeles Chargers used to be known as the San Diego Chargers. The team started out playing in Los Angeles, but they relocated to San Diego in 1961. They later relocated back to Los Angeles. The name was changed back to the Los

Angeles Chargers in 2017. "Chargers" came from a contest that was held by Barron Hilton, the team's first owner. His father, Conrad Hilton, liked "Chargers" because of its association with yelling "charge."

6. Nick Gabaldon was the first surfer of African-American and Latino descent, according to California records. Gabaldon was born in Los Angeles. While he was a recreational surfer, he is often recognized as a huge influencer of African-Americans in the surfing world of California.

7. Mark Spitz was considered the Michael Phelps of his time. Born in Modesto, California, Spitz once won seven gold medals in swimming during one Olympics—a record he held until 2008 when Phelps beat him!

8. Magic Johnson is part owner of the Los Angeles Dodgers. In 2012, Johnson and the team's co-owners paid $2 billion for the team, which is the highest amount of money anyone has ever paid for a professional sports team. As of 2014, Johnson also became co-owner of the Los Angeles Sparks.

9. Former professional boxer Oscar De La Hoya is a Mexican-American who was born in East Los Angeles. He graduated from Garfield High School in East Los Angeles and won an Olympic gold medal in the lightweight division not long after.

10. Former quarterback Warren Moon is a Los Angeles native! He attended Alexandra Hamilton High School. Moon began his professional football career in the Canadian Football League (CFL), where he played for the Edmonton Eskimos. He later went on to play for four NFL teams: the Houston Oilers, Minnesota Vikings, Seattle Seahawks, and Kansas City Chiefs. Moon was inducted into the Pro Football Hall of Fame, making him the first African-American quarterback to ever accomplish that.

11. Former Baltimore Orioles player and Hall of Famer Eddie Murray was born in Los Angeles. Murray went to Locke High School in LA where he played on the baseball team. He batted .500 during his senior year. He was classmates with former St. Louis Cardinals player Ozzie Smith.

12. The Los Angeles Lakers have more Facebook fans than any other sports team in the United States! They're also the NBA team with the highest number of Twitter followers.

13. Cayla Barnes, who plays ice hockey for both Boston College and the American national team, is from California! Barnes was born in Eastvale, California. She played in the 2015, 2016, and 2017 Women's World Championships.

14. In 2012, professional athletes in California paid a

combined $216.8 million in income taxes!

15. The Los Angeles Dodgers weren't originally a California-based baseball team. They were the Brooklyn Dodgers first. The team moved to Los Angeles in 1958 and were renamed the Los Angeles Dodgers.

16. Leigh Steinberg is an American sports agent whose client list has included Troy Aikman, Warren Moon, Ricky Williams, and Oscar De La Hoya. Steinberg, a California native, is said to be the inspiration of the sports agent in the movie *Jerry Maguire*.

17. The San Diego Padres named their team in honor of the former Pacific Coast League minor league team. The minor league Padres was led by Ted Williams. The name, which means "fathers" in Spanish, honors the Spanish founders of San Diego.

18. Sean McVay, head coach of the Los Angeles Rams, set a historical record in 2017 when he became the youngest head coach in the history of the modern NFL. McVay became head coach at just 30 years old.

19. Former NFL player Larry Allen was born in Los Angeles and grew up in Compton. Allen went to four different high schools, spending only one school year at each. These included Centennial

High School for his freshman year, Tokay High School in Lodi for his sophomore year, Edison High School in Stockton, and Vintage High School in Napa. Allen didn't graduate from high school, but he went to Butte College in Oroville where he played on the football team. He later attended Sonoma State University before eventually going on to play for the Dallas Cowboys and the San Francisco 49ers. Throughout the course of his career, Allen played in more Pro Bowls than any other Dallas Cowboy in history. Allen was also inducted into the Pro Football Hall of Fame.

20. The Oakland Raiders are one of only three teams in the NFL that is known not to retire players' jerseys. It's said that the reason is that they believe reusing players' jerseys helps keep their memory alive. The only exception to this rule is 00, a number which was banned by the NFL.

Test Yourself – Questions and Answers

1. Which major surfing competition is held in California every year?

   a. The World Open in Surfing
   b. The U.S. Open in Surfing
   c. The California Open in Surfing

2. Which former NFL player is *not* from California?

   a. Peyton Manning
   b. O.J. Simpson
   c. Larry Allen

3. Which New York Yankees legend is from California?

   a. Babe Ruth
   b. Joe DiMaggio
   c. Lou Gehrig

4. Gene Autry was the first owner of which of California's MLB teams?

   a. Los Angeles Angels
   b. San Diego Padres
   c. Los Angeles Dodgers

5. Which of California's professional sports teams has the most Facebook followers of any sports team in the United States?

   a. Los Angeles Angels
   b. Los Angeles Dodgers
   c. Los Angeles Lakers

Answers

1. b.
2. a.
3. b.
4. a.
5. c.

DON'T FORGET YOUR
FREE BOOKS

GET THEM FOR FREE ON
WWW.TRIVIABILL.COM

OTHER BOOKS IN THIS SERIES

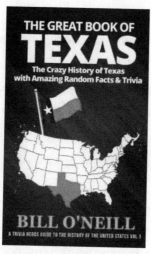

Are you looking to learn more about Texas? Sure, you've heard about the Alamo and JFK's assassination in history class, but there's so much about the Lone Star State that even natives don't know about. In this trivia book, you'll journey through Texas's history, pop culture, sports, folklore, and so much more!

In The Great Book of Texas, some of the things you will learn include:

- Which Texas hero isn't even from Texas?
- Why is Texas called the Lone Star State?
- Which hotel in Austin is one of the most haunted hotels in the United States?
- Where was Bonnie and Clyde's hideout

located?

- Which Tejano musician is buried in Corpus Christi?
- What unsolved mysteries happened in the state?
- Which Texas-born celebrity was voted "Most Handsome" in high school?
- Which popular TV show star just opened a brewery in Austin?

You'll find out the answers to these questions and many other facts. Some of them will be fun, some of them will creepy, and some of them will be sad, but all of them will be fascinating! This book is jampacked with everything you could have ever wondered about Texas.

Whether you consider yourself a Texas pro or you know absolutely nothing about the state, you'll learn something new as you discover more about the state's past, present, and future. Find out about things that weren't mentioned in your history book. In fact, you might even be able to impress your history teacher with your newfound knowledge once you've finished reading! So, what are you waiting for? Dive in now to learn all there is to know about the Lone Star State!

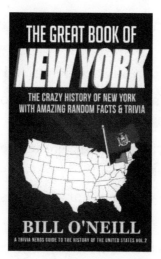

Want to learn more about New York? Sure, you've heard about the Statue of Liberty, but how much do you really know about the Empire State? Do you know why it's even called the Empire State? There's so much about New York that even state natives don't know. In this trivia book, you'll learn more about New York's history, pop culture, folklore, sports, and so much more!

In The Great Book of New York, you'll learn the answers to the following questions:

- Why is New York City called the Big Apple?
- What genre of music started out in New York City?
- Which late actress's life is celebrated at a festival held in her hometown every year?

- Which monster might be living in a lake in New York?

- Was there really a Staten Island bogeyman?

- Which movie is loosely based on New York in the 1800s?

- Which cult favorite cake recipe got its start in New York?

- Why do the New York Yankees have pinstripe uniforms?

These are just a few of the many facts you'll find in this book. Some of them will be fun, some of them will be sad, and some of them will be so chilling they'll give you goosebumps, but all of them will be fascinating! This book is full of everything you've ever wondered about New York.

It doesn't matter if you consider yourself a New York state expert or if you know nothing about the Empire State. You're bound to learn something new as you journey through each chapter. You'll be able to impress your friends on your next trivia night!

So, what are you waiting for? Dive in now so you can learn all there is to know about New York!